# The Salvation Tree

## John Killinger

HARPER & ROW, PUBLISHERS
New York, Evanston, San Francisco, London

234
K48a

FIRST EDITION

Designed by Patricia Dunbar

Library of Congress Cataloging in Publication Data

Killinger, John.
  The salvation tree.

  Includes bibliographical references.
  1. Salvation. 2. Christianity—20th century.
I. Title.
BT751.2.K54   1973        234        72–11357
ISBN 0–06–064583–0

75-3500

# The Salvation Tree

# Contents

# Introduction

   I remember what a simple matter salvation seemed to be when I was a boy growing up in a small town.

   Our preacher was always outlining the "plan" of it, as he called it, in his sermons.

   "All have sinned," he would intone in his cagiest, most sepulchral voice, "and come short of the glory of God." That was from the third chapter of Romans, as everyone knew, and it wasn't just the preacher talking but God himself. You felt a chill as the hand of the Great Magistrate swept the horizon from one side to the other, taking in everybody. The cavernous voice continued, mostly restating and paraphrasing what it had already said, with maybe a few illustrations of our general wickedness thrown in for good measure.

   Then it would shift. No longer ominous and wary, it would suddenly lighten with a note of hope. The Magistrate was about to become conciliatory. He always did. It was expected at this point. "Believe on the Lord Jesus Christ"—he was positively sweet now—"and thou shalt be saved." Sixteenth chapter of Acts —Paul and Barnabas converting the Philippian jailer. Believe and be saved, believe and be saved, believe and be saved. The repetition was by this time almost hypnotic. Who could resist the power? The voice was generous, friendly, cogent. Believe and be saved.

But there was one more step, the voice said. One more easy, important step. "Confess." Romans ten—confessing Jesus before men. Of course it took courage. Who said it didn't? But hadn't Jesus confessed us before his heavenly Father? Ten thousand angels waited at the foot of the pulpit to throw their arms around us as we came forward to confess. The voice was low and pleading. Who could resist? After all, it was God's plan, not man's. We couldn't believe it if it was just the preacher saying it. But it wasn't. It was God.

We stood and sang. "Just as I am, without one plea, but that thy blood was shed for me." The preacher, one arm high in the air, palm toward the congregation and fingers spread wide, wooed us in a loud voice right along with the music. Wouldn't some lost soul come home, come home? Sometimes one did, or two, and the preacher would come down from the pulpit to welcome them. We never saw the angels, but we felt them and our hearts soared. "O Lamb of God, I come, I come."

As I say, it was simple then. The fountain square, graced by an ivy-covered courthouse and a dinky fountain that no longer worked, was the center of the world. I once heard a candidate for governor speak there. Pep rallies for the high-school football team were held there. The band played there for heroes returning from the war. Those were the days when anybody who came back was a hero.

But a lot has happened since then. In fact, a lot had happened before that that I didn't know about. The world was already on its way to becoming more complicated than I could imagine.

And so was I.

I still go back to the fountain square occasionally. It isn't the center of the world any more. It isn't even the center of town. A four-lane bypass and two or three new shopping centers have left it all but deserted.

Sometimes I wonder, when I go back, if it is the center of the world to anybody growing up there. Maybe it is to some. But surely not the way it was to me. Not since the shopping centers and television and the age of travel.

I am always amazed, wherever I go—London, Paris, Copenhagen—at the number of American teenagers roaming the streets. Over there by themselves. No hours to keep, no guardians to report to, no restrictions whatever. Free. And knowledgeable.

Many of the preachers, I understand, still talk about the plan of salvation the way preachers used to. Some of the illustrations are different. There are allusions now to Buchenwald and My Lai and nuclear power and astronauts and the ecological crisis. But the abecedarian approach is essentially the same.

How can they do it, I wonder? How do they make it work?

Maybe—I often come round to this conclusion—it does still work at a certain stage of one's development, regardless of the shape the world is in. Maybe there is something so fundamental about the old message and the ritual of conversion itself that it will always be valid for many people.

Surely the Jesus Movement today is evidence of that. Ninety-eight percent of its constituency were born after 1950. Children of the technological culture.

"Believe and confess" as a way of life.

But it isn't all that simple any more. Not for me, and not for a lot of people. Life is too diverse, and salvation too complicated, to be reduced to a formula. We feel uneasy with the reductionism of the old preaching, as though it ignored too much to be true. We are not keen to undermine the faith of those whose belief is simple, for most of us remember when ours was. But neither do we want to close our own doors to faith because belief is no longer simple for us. That is an option to which we cannot afford to surrender. We are not willing to accept that either/or—either we believe very simply, even naïvely, or we reject Christianity entirely.

## A Modern Parable

This book is about salvation. Not about how simple it is, but about how complex it is. It isn't intended to convert anybody. It is intended as a kind of overview of some of the thinking about salvation that is going on among those for whom belief is no longer easy, simple, or black and white.

Its title is frankly derived from a central image in the play which for many critics marked the beginning of the postmodern era in the theater—Samuel Beckett's *Waiting for Godot.* You will recall that play. It is a puzzling piece—as so many things are today. And it is spare, without much scenery or action.

There are two acts.

In the beginning we meet the two principal characters. Estragon and Vladimir. They call each other Gogo and Didi.

The only scenery is a withered old tree without any leaves. The critics have made a lot of this. They say it represents all the special trees in human history—the Bodhi tree of Buddhism, the Cross of Jesus, Yggdrasill, the legendary tree of life, and many others.

Gogo and Didi's dialogue is pretty disjointed. As in ordinary speech off the stage, much of the communication occurs nonverbally, through gesture and mime or through prior understanding and association.

Interestingly, the two men have not been on stage long before they begin to talk about the Bible. Didi asks if Gogo remembers the Gospels. Gogo says he remembers the maps of the Holy Land.

A short time later, Didi asks if he remembers the two thieves. Gogo doesn't. Didi asks if he should tell him about them. Gogo says no. Didi says it will pass the time.

But here we should sample the flavor of the text.

VLADIMIR: It'll pass the time. *(Pause.)* Two thieves, crucified at the same time as our Saviour. One—

ESTRAGON: Our what?

VLADIMIR: Our Saviour. Two thieves. One is supposed to have been saved and the other . . . *(he searches for the contrary of saved)* . . . damned.

ESTRAGON: Saved from what?

VLADIMIR: Hell.

ESTRAGON: I'm going. *(He does not move.)*[1]

There follows an extended discussion of the thieves and the fact that only one of the four Gospels alludes to one thief's being saved. Didi is puzzled by the fact that two of the Gospels don't mention the thieves at all, while a third says that both thieves abused Jesus. Gogo is bored by the whole subject. Eventually they drop it and talk about what they are doing where they are.

Didi says they are waiting for Godot. As it turns out, of course, they don't really know Godot and aren't fully certain that that is his name. They aren't even positive that this is the place where he said to meet him, or that it is time for him to be there. They simply wait, and try to occupy their time by talking or playing little games.

One critic has said that *Waiting for Godot* is a play in which "nothing happens—*twice,*" because there are two acts. Curiously, though, there is one notable difference when the curtain goes up on the second act. The withered tree has four or five leaves on it.

It is impossible to say why. Perhaps it is because a couple of strange visitors came by in the first act. Or because the two characters have tried to hang themselves on it at the end of the act.

Once, in the second act, they become excited because they think Godot is coming.

1. Samuel Beckett, *Waiting for Godot* (New York: Grove Press, 1954), p. 9.

"It's Godot!" shouts Didi. "At last! Gogo! It's Godot! We're saved!"

They race around frenziedly looking for him.

Gogo says, "I'm in hell!"

The search fails to produce anyone. Finally they sit down and watch. Silence.

Vladimir says, "You must have had a vision."

At the end of the play, either Godot has not come or the two men have not recognized him. Gogo says he can't go on like this. Didi says they will hang themselves tomorrow, unless Godot comes.

"And if he comes?" asks Gogo.

"We'll be saved," says Didi.

Beckett himself has denied repeatedly that he intended the name Godot as a theological symbol meaning "the diminutive God." Yet people persist in saying that is what the play is really about. Its whole undertone seems to refer to the spiritual malaise of our time. It recalls an earlier age when being saved or damned was a clear and simple matter based on the biblical accounts of sin and redemption. Only now, in this present time, many persons no longer understand it the same way. Their lives are fragmented and diffuse, like Didi's and Gogo's. God is not so clear as he formerly was. They halfway expect him, but don't know when or where or how. They know that if he comes they'll be saved. But their confidence in his coming is shaky.

Salvation is consequently less clear and sure than it was. Like millions of people the world over, the two men occupy themselves with little games to fend off boredom and to pass the time. Whatever salvation they enjoy is of a limited and temporary sort. Life is no different at the end of the play than it was in the beginning. They have only succeeded in getting through a few more hours. Their existence is still uncentered.

## Secular Forms of Salvation

One significant fact to be noted in this very contemporary play is that salvation is still a crucial matter to man, whether he understands the term in former ways or not. Even if talk about the thief on the cross is strange and distant to him, the long entanglement of Christianity and Western culture has left its imprint on his unconscious. He wants to be saved, to be redeemed, to be delivered. Why, or from what, or *to* what, may not be certain to him. God may have become vague and remote, like Godot. But the desire for salvation lingers like a shadow in the mind.

Many of us can identify with this. Even if our fountain squares and religious experiences lie now in our personal Dark Ages, we cannot shake the feeling that something must be done to save the world. We are committed to the idea of redemption. Maybe we didn't make the commitment, but it was made for us. The notion of being saved has become endemic in our very culture. It flows in our bloodstream.

Recently I asked a group of adults in a suburban church to do a bit of brainstorming. "I want you to think of some words that come into your head when I mention 'salvation,' " I said. "Don't sweat it. Just relax and say whatever comes to mind." As they said the words that popped into their heads, I wrote them down on a chalkboard.

Here is the list, without any editing:

> Evangelism
> Revival
> Sawdust trail
> Encounter groups
> Psychoanalysis
> Jesus
> Health spas
> Tennis

Insurance
Ecology
Church
Orphanages
Daycare centers
Medical clinics
Organic foods
Yoga
Gurus
H.E.W.
Education
Vocational training
O.E.O.
Rehabilitation
Social Security
Welfare
NAACP
Councils on the Arts
Movies
Technology
Retardation centers
Family planning centers
Psychic phenomena

Some of the terms were doubtless produced by association with those that preceded them. But the remarkable thing is the diversity of items these suburbanites associated with salvation. Once we got beyond some rather immediate word associations, such as "evangelism" and "revival," all kinds of nonchurchy relationships became apparent. Most of the items, in fact, refer to councils or programs which have become part of our everyday existence.

I asked the group if they really associated human salvation with these extraecclesiastical organizations. The consensus was that they did not normally think of them in this way, and that they still regarded the Church as the institution most basically involved in salvation, but that they did view the organizations and programs as "spin-offs" from the Church's concern for mankind.

Would they concede, speaking only for themselves, that salvation had to do with much more than man's soul? Yes, if by "soul" was meant some nebulous inner spirit separable from the remainder of the person. Salvation, they were all agreed, involved much more than a momentary conversion experience; it had as much to do with total human environment as with personal ecstasy.

Did this mean that salvation, in their minds, was as important for their lives now as for any prospect of an afterlife? Yes, certainly it was. Some felt that it had to do only with this life. Others were reluctant to go so far, but thought of it as of about equal importance to this life and another. The members of the group clearly indicated that the Christian faith, for them, is not a means of escaping the burdens of life; on the contrary, they see it as a means of fulfilling life in the world.

## The Movement to Celebration

This shift, I am convinced, is becoming more and more universal. It is a shift from the *temporal* to the *spatial* aspects of salvation. People were once concerned to escape from the tyranny of time in their lives. Their existence was uncertain, often terminated abruptly by disease or violence. Moreover, it was frequently lived under adverse circumstances: poverty, squalor, and even slavery were the lot of the majority. It was natural, therefore, to envision redemption as an afterlife in which all wrongs and inequities would be redressed. The world was a place of trial; *heaven* was man's home.

Now, in our part of the world (though things remain often pretty brutal elsewhere) life doesn't seem quite so cruel and uncertain any more. The rampages of pain and disease and untimely death have been vastly mitigated. The grim reaper no longer seems so grim.

Consequently we think less than our fathers did about escaping into another world. We are much more concerned about the world at hand. The old puritanical fear of the world is being replaced by a mood of celebration. "Touch not, taste not" is giving way to "Touch and taste everything!" Many ministers are taking their sermon texts from the book of Genesis, with its emphasis on the goodness of Creation, instead of from Revelation, where Rome is a harlot and human life is portrayed in its decadence. Occupying the earth, the space God has given us has become the ultimate goal of life.

The question "What if there is no life after death?" has given way to "What if there is no life *before* death?

The former celebrations of the Church, with high festivals and colorful pageants, were bent on sanctifying men's lives for life after death. Everything existed for the world to come, of which this world was deemed a poor, imperfect shadow.

The kind of celebration sweeping the Church today, however, exults in the here and now. It elevates small moments, ordinary events, and unlikely people and gives thanks for them. It appreciates things as they are, not as they might become.

As Ross Snyder says, "Contemporary celebration roots itself in lived moments. We are not celebrating cloud nine or our own emotions, or how sensational we feel when we 'let go.' We are celebrating a reality which we find at work in our world at particular points in very concrete encounters. We are transforming epochal events into meanings and the culture of a people."[2]

One result of the new celebrative mood is an entirely new kind of devotional literature in our time. Until only a few years ago, devotional books were primly bound little tomes like *The Imitation of Christ* or *Streams in the Desert*. The very typography was

2. Ross Snyder, *Contemporary Celebration* (New York: Abingdon Press, 1971), p. 10.

a giveaway. Usually the initial letters were Gothic or Old English. Sometimes the entire texts were composed in those stiltedly dignified "spiritual" types.

But no more! Now they come in all sizes, shapes, and colors. They are jam-packed with vibrancy and life. Photographs abound, mostly with a high degree of sensitivity for human hands and faces, for trees and flowers and windswept prairies—even for sidewalks, tenements, and vacant lots. The shift is dramatic. Now it is the world that is seen as the arena of God's presence. Not some sugary, vaguely imaginable otherworld, but the very world where we are born, attend school, make love, work, and die.

Whether we realize it or not, a basic change has occurred and is still occurring in our theological perspective. It is becoming harder and harder for us to picture God as being "up there" or "out there," managing heaven like some fantastic, ethereal circus tent and occasionally interrupting the laws of nature in some special attempt to divert a few more lost souls under the flap that leads to the center ring. The "God is dead" theology which was making the headlines a few years ago was one sign of the change. It introduced a new candor into Church affairs, so that rank-and-file believers could stop perjuring themselves by confessing to all kinds of beliefs and doctrines they could not hold with any sense of reality.

We live in a new era, and new eras require new assessments of old ideas.

### The Freedom to Change

This book, as I said, is about salvation. It is an attempt to reassess an old idea, the one that has been most central to the origin and history of Christianity.

In a sense, it is a personal pilgrimage—an effort to get from the fountain square to the Sea of Tranquility, from the plan of salvation as I heard it in my adolescence to the War on Poverty, the Peace

Movement, Women's Liberation, Earth Day, and all the other aspects of life-redemption I believe in today, and to have some idea when I am through what the relationship between the two points really is.

But I am convinced it is not my pilgrimage alone. There are many others who are trying to make it just as I am. For their sakes, I should include some word about the order of the trek—that is, about the plan of the book.

First we must examine the idea of salvation as it occurs in the Bible. This is not a simple matter, for we carry many preconceptions to the Bible when we go to read it. As Kierkegaard said, we talk about reading the scriptures, but they usually read us by revealing our prejudices. But we must try anyway, for there is where our story begins.

Then we shall make a whirlwind journey through the history of the Church and what it has had to say about salvation. Does it surprise us that it has not always said the same thing, but has varied according to the times and their philosophies? It shouldn't. After all, everything we know is conditioned by everything else we know. Move a few trees around, and the whole landscape looks different.

After that, we shall attempt to isolate some of the most prominent factors in salvation thinking today, such as education, technology, human engineering, psychology, group dynamics, psychosomatics, and sociopolitical revolution, and deal with them at some length. All these factors, it should be noted, have to do with reshaping the present world we live in.

It is in these latter chapters that it really hits the fan. They are *secular* components of our redemption philosophy, and sometimes they cut directly across the religious components. Is it possible to work out some kind of *entente cordiale* between the two or are they bound to remain enemies?

Finally, in a sort of "Where do we go from here?" chapter, I have attempted to answer this question. But note that I have slipped from using the editorial "we" into the first person singular. It is the route *my* pilgrimage takes; it may not be yours. For here is where it becomes most personal, when we try to put the scraps together to make a whole, to fashion a *modus vivendi,* a life-style for our time. At this point the reader is invited to be most careful, lest he exchange one set of beliefs that were never really his, intimately and profoundly, for another set of the same.

And now, lest the pilgrimage seem too effortless at any stage, let me enter one more warning note.

We never quite transcend our beginnings. Regardless of how much cultural patterns, including traditional religious thought, become eroded, they continue to influence our thinking and behavior for many years to come. We may think we have left behind old habits of mind, only to see them emerge, in some moment of crisis, stronger than ever. As recent studies of death and dying indicate, for example, persons who receive strict religious indoctrination about sin and guilt in their youth, then live apparently liberated, carefree lives as adults, often revert to a sense of guilt and fear of religious punishment when faced with approaching death. The trauma of mortality acts as a trigger to release feelings and emotions buried for years in the subconscious mind.

This is one of the profound insights of Beckett's *Godot.* Didi and Gogo are modern men, inhabitants of a modern wasteland. They know very little about the Bible and even less about the Church. Yet they are haunted by an earlier age's sense of miracle and redemption. The center of their uncenteredness, if we may call it that, is the wretched old tree. They never leave it—raising the speculation that perhaps they cannot. They say they are waiting for Godot. Even though they have not seen him and are not sure they would recognize him if they did—Why? They are themselves unaware of the reason. Somehow the past is still a part of them, still nags them, even though they are creatures of another time and place.

Thus, Beckett appears to be saying, our yesterdays always pursue us.

It would be foolish, then, to suppose that any of the aspects of the redemption picture discussed in this book have actually replaced Western man's former notions of salvation. It is more accurate to say that they now coexist with the former notions and that there is even an interplay between them, an interplay which sometimes eludes or defies analysis.

We should not, on that account, fear to acknowledge or even to enjoy the interplay. Faith, after all, is open, dynamic, growing, not closed and fearful. It is future-oriented. All the great heroes of Judaism and Christianity have been bold, iconoclastic persons who were not content to remain in the past. Their stories are stories of risk, adventure, and change.

It is easy enough to enslave ourselves to the past and the way things have always been done. There is a feeling of security in doing this. But we ought not to rationalize our own fears and insecurities by pretending we support the past for its own sake.

The genius of Christianity, from Jesus on, has always been its newness, its freedom, its readiness to read the signs of the times, and its willingness to believe that religion was made for man, not man for religion.

# 1

# Variations on a Biblical Theme

Salvation, though not exclusively the property of the Jews, is a major biblical theme. We might almost say, in fact, that the Bible is *obsessed* by the idea of being saved.

To understand this we have only to look at the contemporary nation of Israel and see how precarious is her location among the other nations of the world. It was even more so in the days of the old trade routes, when there were no airplanes and whatever armies or merchantile caravans passing from East to West or West to East had to cross her borders to get where they were going. Struggle and exile were to be dominant motifs in her national memory. And rescue. Rescue was especially important to a nation so small and friendless.

For such a people, so dangerously and yet so defiantly situated, where was rescue likely to come from? The psalmist spoke for more than himself when he let his eyes trace the rocky terrain and said, "I will lift up mine eyes unto the hills, from whence cometh my help; my help cometh from the Lord, which made heaven and earth."[1]

1. King James Version. In general, scriptural quotations in this volume are from the New English Bible unless otherwise noted.

Only the Lord could be faithful in such a situation.

Correspondingly, salvationism as a religious manifestation flourished along the American frontier, where life was fraught with danger and disease. The evangelists found a ready audience among people whose small personal empires were a constant prey to scalawags and militant tribesmen. The government was rarely near enough to help when they needed it. Their help too was from the Lord.

There are sociologists who speculate that revival fires in this country are still nourished by a residual sense of insecurity or desperation stemming from those earlier days. Fundamentalism, which feeds mainly on immigrants and blue-collar families, plays the insecurity angle to the hilt in order to introduce the *deus ex machina* of divine salvation. Billy Graham's standard sermon opener is a citation of the evils and uncertainties abroad in the land, usually bolstered by the day's newspaper headlines or the warning of some prominent figure. Even the Jesus Movement and Campus Crusade, which often appeal to children of the upper classes, depend heavily on a mood of disillusionment and transitoriness to produce disciples for their chauvinistic, emotionally unbalanced programs.

It is easy to see, in these terms, why history—or historical criticism—is regarded by many evangelicals as the enemy of faith. It insists on reminding us of certain psychological or sociological factors that contributed to, or at least help to account for, what has happened in a given time and place. It humanizes the past by removing its veil of mystery and ignorance and offering a rational interpretation of it.

My preacher who held court two blocks off the Fountain Square every Sunday was innocent of history. That is, he was innocent of history when it came to reading the Bible. Otherwise, he professed a great love for it and was constantly citing edifying bits of information from the past. But when he talked about the Bible his sense of history simply deserted him. It was as if everything in it had either happened or been said all at the same time, under the same set of conditions. Not only that, but it was all coextensive with our own time. Salvation was all of a piece. It always had been and always would be. Believe and confess. That was the eternal plan.

But the Bible, I was subsequently to discover, is not all of a piece. Anything but! Even some of its single books are not all of a piece. Isaiah, for example, is now known to have been written by at least three different authors living in three different periods. The whole of the Bible stretches over centuries, with multiple influences and borrowings at every stage. And to read any theme in it as if it were perfectly continuous, all on a single level of meaning, is—well, fatuous and irresponsible to say the least.

I will give my preacher this much: the salvation theme is constant in the scriptures. It does not always mean the same thing, but it is almost always there. The incredible fact, given the diverse authorship and span of composition, is not that there is so little unity in what the scriptures deal with, but that there is so much. I can understand how my preacher conflated everything. It probably never occurred to him not to.

What we must do now is to make some effort to *un*conflate the scriptures—pull them apart a little, and get some historical perspective on what salvation probably meant to people at various stages of national and individual consciousness. To do this we have to go behind the scenes and ask what was happening there that would help us to realize how those responsible for various biblical passages about salvation understood their own sayings.

**The People of the Land**

Since the earliest days of the Jews, there have been two focal points in their thinking: a land and a people. Around these two centers have converged all their hopes and dreams. Some say these are not two centers but one: the land and the people are a single entity.

The real beginning of the Old Testament, say many scholars, is not the book of Genesis, but this little passage from the fifteenth chapter of the book of Exodus:

And Miriam the prophetess, Aaron's sister, took up her tambourine, and all the women followed her, dancing to the sound of the tambourines; and Miriam sang them this refrain:

> Sing to the Lord, for he has risen up in triumph;
> the horse and his rider he has hurled into the sea.

The horse and the rider refer to the Egyptian armies that drowned in the Red Sea while pursuing their rebellious Israelite slaves. Here, say the scholars, is the point at which Israel truly became a nation. Before that there had been only nomadic tribesmen and a race of slaves. Now there was a people suddenly made self-conscious—conscious of their identity—by a miraculous delivery from bondage and death.

Later they would spin tales of their ancestry, and some of their number, relying partly on inventive genius and partly on borrowed mythologies and legends, would trace their lineage back to the Garden of Eden and a special act of divine creation. But their real moment of passage, when they actually became a nation with political reality, was when their scouts raced up to report what had befallen the pursuing horsemen and they knew they were free.

"Exodus," which means "the way out," became a dominant note in all later Jewish theology. God was the God of deliverance, and they were the people of his greatest act of deliverance. Forever after, even in the detention camps of Germany and the *stetls* of Russia, they would sing of that moment and pray for its reenactment.

Once they were free, of course, the land soon became important to them. Although their grandfathers had been nomads, they were themselves unsuited to such an existence. Quarreling broke out among them, and they complained that they had been brought into the wilderness to starve. Several things kept them going during these first crucial years as a nation. One was the sternness and sagacity of their leaders. Another was the remarkable code of laws they developed for handling their internal disputes and regulating their daily behavior. But probably the most important thing was the promise of a land. Their Deliverer would not leave them homeless. He was leading them to a land which he would give them—a land reported to be unbelievably rich and productive, where each tribe would have its own territory and each man his herds and garden. They were like the settlers in our own wilderness who forded swollen streams, crossed treacherous mountain passes, and braved weather, disease, and bloody attacks for the dream of farmlands and mineral lodes at the end of the journey. The promise and the hope kept them alive when nothing else would.

Once they had taken the land from the Canaanites and other tribes that occupied it when they arrived, the Jews never ceased to identify themselves with it. However many times they were defeated in battle and carried into exile, they always struggled to go back. The identification between them and their part of the earth was sacred. The God who had rescued them from slavery had given it to them. The rescue and the land constituted them a people. Nor have four thousand years changed things, as even the most casual observer of Zionism knows. They are the people of the land.

It is no wonder, then, that the classic notion of salvation in the Old Testament has to do with the people and the land. Salvation there is primarily corporate, not individual, and pertains to the fullness of life on earth—not to an otherworldly existence in a time beyond time. Maybe persons with large, intimately related families can understand this today; the welfare of the individual is dependent on the general welfare of all. But most of us, lacking close, extended families, must make a real effort to understand it. We are much more accustomed to thinking and acting as isolated individuals. We speak of the *uniqueness* of each person or soul. But the very word for "soul" in Hebrew—*nephesh*—conveyed a sense of relationships the person was dependent on. The soul was a network of beings and things. A man's wife was part of his soul. So were his children and cattle. If anything belonging to him was harmed or taken away, it affected his soul.

The story of Job, whose origins doubtless predate the Jewish nation, is an illustration. Job's soul was healthy in the beginning, but it descended nearly to death when he lost everything. He complained that his life was only a vapor, that in his weakened condition it was better to be dead, to enter into Sheol, that gloomy region of ultimate powerlessness from which no man returns. In the end, however, he submitted to God in repentance and God restored his fortunes, doubling all his possessions, including sons and daughters. His soul, once faint, became strong again.

Because his own identity was so inextricably linked to that of the Hebrew people, every Jew regarded his salvation as dependent on the condition of all Jews. The health of the nation was essential to the well-being of the individual. This is why the kingdom of David became so inseparably a part of the idea of salvation: to be a Jew in the reign of David was the highest spiritual state to which a Jew could aspire. Exile from Israel on the other hand, has always meant spiritual attrition or weakness.

The kingdom the Jews wanted was never a heavenly kingdom —not, at least, in the spiritualized sense. The Old Testament bears witness to their strong sense of the goodness of the earth, especially of that portion of the earth which God swore to give his people. Deliverance might refer to all kinds of freeing acts—to being freed from illness, from creditors, or from persecutors. But its ultimate reference was always to the freed nation, the freed people of God, inhabiting their own land and living out in joyous fulfillment the covenant given to their fathers.

Salvation was of the earth earthy, in the highest sense of the word.

## The Rise of Apocalyptic

But the land God gave to the Hebrews was not well located for peaceful fulfillment. It was, on the contrary, right on the road to everywhere. It became a perennial battleground, with nation after nation contesting for the right to occupy it. The Jews could not hold it forever.

Given their sense of identification with the land, they might have reacted in either of two ways to the long centuries of occupation by enemy forces, desolation by war, even exile.

They could have said to themselves, "Look, maybe our fathers thought the Almighty willed them this troublesome burden of ground, but they were wrong. The covenant was all in their minds. They believed because they wanted to believe. We are foolish to persist in their belief. It is time we stopped fantasizing and faced facts." Some Jews doubtless responded to their situation in this manner. There are references in the Old Testament to those who followed no longer in the way of their fathers. In our own time, a similar argument forms the basis of Richard Rubenstein's book *After Auschwitz*. Who, asks Rubenstein, after the deaths of millions of Jews in Nazi Germany, can seriously believe any longer in a God who is reputed to favor Jewish people?

But a second reaction was also possible. That was to intensify the vision of what had been promised to the Jews and to preach that vision as something yet to be fulfilled in a manner beyond even the wildest dreams of the average Jew. There are Zionists today who fervently cling to such a vision, expecting God to interrupt the normal historical process and vindicate their people's centuries of suffering and hope.

It is this second reaction that is most relevant to the history of salvation thought, for it reshaped the classic pattern of the understanding of salvation, the one described earlier, and served as a bridge between it and the way Jesus and the early Christians understood it.

We may call this intensifying or transmuting of the original vision by its technical name: apocalyptic. The word is from the Greek *apocalyptein,* which means to "uncover" or "reveal." It is used by scholars for a certain pattern of writings or sayings in which the understanding of God's covenant with the Jews is radicalized to the point where he is expected to intervene suddenly in world affairs and transfigure all history, establishing Jerusalem as the glorious center of the nations. The "uncovering" or "revealing" relates to God's having revealed the vision to a prophet or servant who transmits it to the faithful.

There are evidences that the apocalyptic genre flourished during the centuries immediately before the time of Christ, and of course portions of both Old and New Testament were influenced by it. Isaiah 24–27, Zechariah 12–14, Ezekiel 37–39, and the book of Daniel are all written in the apocalyptic idiom, as are various sections of Mark and Matthew and the book of Revelation.

The features of apocalyptic vary somewhat among particular examples, but several are rather persistent. The language tends to be very dramatic and to speak either openly or symbolically of an impending catastrophe known as the Day of the Lord. Only God himself knows when that day will be, but the signs indicate that it is imminent. When it occurs, the present power arrangements will be abrogated; earthly rulers will be toppled and the evil forces they served will be bound or destroyed. Then God's little ones, his faithful servants who have not forsaken the covenant he made with their fathers, will be set in high places.

Some apocalypses spoke of a Messiah or Anointed One whom God would send to lead his people in that day and who would be enthroned in the new Kingdom after the fashion of David. The Kingdom of this new leader, however, would no longer be subject to the woes of the kingdoms men have previously known. There would be no more enmity or war. The Messiah would reign forever.

Another important feature of some apocalyptic literature was the teaching of a future life for those who were already dead. In Daniel 12:1–2 (NEB), for example, we read:

> At that moment [the time of the end] Michael shall appear,
> Michael the great captain,
> who stands guard over your fellow-countrymen;
> and there will be a time of distress
> such as has never been
> since they became a nation till that moment.
> But at that moment your people will be delivered,
> every one who is written in the book:
> many of those who sleep in the dust of the earth will wake,
> some to everlasting life
> and some to the reproach of eternal abhorrence.

This contrasts markedly with the idea of death found in the earlier historical and wisdom literature of the Old Testament, where there was no thought whatsoever of any future existence. But the idea that there would be such a general resurrection at the time of the end had great significance in the teaching of Jesus and the early Church, as we shall see later.

Obviously, the apocalyptic sayings were a way of triumphing over the actual historical situation in which the Jews found themselves. It enabled them to continue, albeit almost fanatically, in the belief that the covenant of God would truly be fulfilled and that justice would be done on earth.

It is important to remember that apocalyptic thought did not remove the faithful's attention from the earth and transfer it to some unearthly or heavenly locale. It called for a new earth, or a transformed earth, but it never actually posited a spiritualized realm existing over against the earth. Even the book of Revelation, which was written near the end of the first century A.D., essentially envisions a renewed earthly kingdom. It speaks of "a new heaven and a new earth," but the writer's vision of heaven is primarily metaphorical; it does not really transfer the scene of human existence from the earth to a spectral realm elsewhere. The Fourth Gospel, which was also written rather late in New Testament times, admits of some confusion in the matter when it represents Jesus as saying that he goes away to prepare a place for us. But the Synoptic Gospels, the book of Acts, and the writings of Paul are univocal in their expectation that the earth itself will be transformed for the habitation of the faithful.

What effect, in summary, did the rise of apocalyptic have on the classic doctrine of salvation? At first, probably very little. Salvation was still basically spatial and corporate in nature. It involved the overthrow of alien powers, the return of the Promised Land to the Jews (especially the faithful Jews), and the reinstatement of the Community of God or the old theocracy under a divinely appointed king. The greater effect was a long-range one, especially in the Christian community. When the apocalyptic expectations of the early Church for an imminent Day of the Lord failed, the symbolism of apocalyptic facilitated the rise of spiritualistic interpretations explaining the goal of the faithful in *otherworldly* terms. It is possible to see the beginnings of this otherworldliness already in late New Testament writings such as the Fourth Gospel, the Letter to the Hebrews, and the book of Revelation. By the time of the first Church council meetings, when the

Jewish beginnings of Christianity were all but forgotten by Gentile philosophers and theologians, there was little talk of inhabiting the earth; heaven had become the object of the Christian's longings. There continued to be speculation as to how heaven was related to the reconstituted earth which the Bible spoke of in connection with the end of all things. But the locus of spiritual attention had clearly undergone a major transition. The Christian, it was emphasized, was only a pilgrim in the earth, looking for the city "not made by hands."

Salvation had become redemption *from* the earth and its sufferings, and was no longer redemption *to* the earth and its joys.

### Jesus as an Apocalyptist

Most of us tend, at this distance from the events and teachings associated with the rise of Christianity, to conflate those events and teachings. We telescope them so drastically that we lose any sense of their own inner conflict and development. Yet we should remember what differences in atmosphere and understanding a mere decade can introduce in human affairs, especially if it is a decade of kaleidoscopic world happenings. Think, for example, of the alterations in public opinion and individual life-style which occurred in the 1960s. In our own country alone during that period television became a major political factor, the black revolution took place, there were at least three important assassinations, the entire educational system underwent significant fluctuations, drugs became a problem of alarming proportions, and for the first time our nation demonstrated popular repudiation of a foreign war in which it was engaged. To be sure, the pace of life is much accelerated today. But the events of the New Testament, and the literature about those events spanned a period of time conservatively estimated at sixty-five years.

Jesus' own ministry is usually regarded as having covered three years' time, although some scholars today believe that to be a very minimal estimate. Considering the dramatic changes which have occurred in the lives and thinking of certain public figures we could name when they came under the pressure of general attention, we ought to have our antennae out to detect possible changes in his attitudes and especially in his conception of his own role as Messiah, to the extent that we are able to speculate on the basis of the scriptures and the scholarship about them.

Scholarly debate over any reconstruction of the life and teachings of Jesus—even over the possibility of such a reconstruction —will go on for decades and even centuries to come. But one thing appears to be fairly clear at this point, namely, that we must be more careful than we have been to remember that Jesus was a Palestinian Jew and that the frame of reference for his thought and ministry was necessarily Jewish. In terms of the understanding of salvation, he can be expected to reflect a Jewish way of thinking. The New Testament writings which cast salvation talk in a Greek or Hellenistic frame of reference tend to represent later interpretations or embellishments.

For our purposes here, it will be helpful to reexamine the portrait of Jesus' ministry and teachings in one of the two Gospels which bear a strong Jewish flavor, Mark and Matthew. Luke-Acts, of course, was written from a Gentile perspective, and the Fourth Gospel was written much later and from an obviously Hellenistic viewpoint. Because Mark is briefer and appears to bear less evidence of arbitrary restructuring than Matthew, we shall take a quick look at the clues it provides to Jesus' understanding of the nature of his work and the salvation which would result from it.

To begin with, there is no account in Mark of a miraculous birth. Instead, the Gospel simply begins with an allusion to John the Baptist and his promise of the coming of One who would baptize his followers in the Holy Spirit (1:1–8). Then Jesus appears at the Jordan and is baptized by John, whereupon the Spirit descends on him from heaven and a voice from the clouds announces that

Jesus is his son. The Spirit immediately sends Jesus away to the wilderness to be tried (1:12–13).

The important thing here is that Jesus came to the messiahship as any other Jew might have come to it, from an anonymous background. God set his approval on him much as he had earlier set his approval on Gideon or Saul or David. The Spirit was not an extension of Jesus's own person, as the Fourth Gospel implies, but was at work in the world independent of Jesus. Jesus, moreover, was sent off to be tried for his faithfulness as any man might be who was selected for an important work.

Later, when John has been arrested by Herod, Jesus comes into the picture again, this time preaching "the Gospel of God" (note that it was not "the Gospel of Christ"), namely: "The time has come; the kingdom of God is upon you; repent, and believe the Gospel" (1:14–15). Here, in this brief sentence, is the entire theme of the ministry of Jesus in the Gospel of Mark. The time has come, the kingdom is breaking upon the world, men had better repent and believe. Jesus is an apocalyptist. That is, he is unveiling a vision of the end of all things and the reordering of the world.

As Jesus goes about proclaiming this "gospel," strange things happen. Demons recognize him and bow down before him. The infirm and the sick are healed. The dead are raised. But citation of these occurrences is offered with a different purpose than in the Fourth Gospel, where much is made of their being "signs" of Jesus' power and authority to an unbelieving world. In Mark they seem to happen for no hortatory or homiletical reason—they do not become the basis for men's belief. Instead, they occur as a kind of discharge of power, like static released by the overlapping of the existing age and the new one that is coming, which is actually present in the Christ himself.

Contrary to the impression other Gospels give, that Jesus tried to persuade others to enter the new Kingdom, Mark pictures him as wishing to keep the Kingdom a secret from most men, or at least to keep the evidences of it which might persuade them to enter it a secret. Over and over, he asks those who are healed or forgiven not to tell anyone (for example. 1:40–45; 7:36; 8:22–26). He even instructs the disciples, when they have confessed that he is the Anointed One, not to tell anyone (8:30), and later, after the transfiguration episode, he urges them not to tell anyone about it "until the Son of Man had risen from the dead" (9:9).

Mark also gives us a perspective on Jesus' use of parables which is not broached at all in the Gospel of Luke. In Luke, the parables are teaching devices whereby Jesus involves his hearers in stories which carry them to sometimes startling conclusions. But Mark explicitly represents Jesus as saying that he uses parables so that those who are not already aware of the Kingdom cannot understand.

When he was alone, the Twelve and others who were round him questioned him about the parables. He replied, "To you the secret of the kingdom of God has been given; but to those who are outside everything comes by way of parables, so that (as Scripture says) they may look and look, but see nothing; they may hear and hear, but understand nothing; otherwise they might turn to God and be forgiven." (4:10–12)

Does this seem strangely contradictory of the general impressions we have held of Jesus as a benevolent Savior intent on gathering everyone to his bosom? If it does, that is because we have elided the accounts of him presented by the Gospels. In Mark, he is a product of Jewish culture and sees both himself and his work in terms of Jewish apocalyptic expectations.

His task is to proclaim the New Age and to gather into the Kingdom those who respond readily to the message that it is arriving. He calls disciples who are fishermen and tells them that they will be fishers of men—they will cast their nets into the tides of the aeons and draw out whatever they catch. When one disciple reports that someone unknown to the band is driving out devils in Jesus' name, Jesus says to let him alone, that—in effect —the tides are flowing (9:38–41).

Mark's Jesus obviously expected the end of all things to come soon. In 9:1 he says to the disciples, "I tell you this: there are some of those standing here who will not taste death before they have seen the kingdom of God already come in power." In 13:28–31, as part of the chapter sometimes referred to as the "Little Apocalypse," Jesus says, "Learn a lesson from the fig-tree. When its tender shoots appear and are breaking into leaf, you know that summer is near. In the same way, when you see all this happening, you may know that the end is near, at the very door. I tell you this: the present generation will live to see it all. Heaven and earth will pass away; my words will never pass away."

Considering this reference to the fig tree, it is possible to interpret 11:12–14, the so-called "cursing of the fig tree" episode, as mere narrative not involving a curse. That is, Jesus, finding no fruit on the tree he passed on the way from Bethany to Jerusalem, may only have said that it wouldn't have any fruit on it again because of the shortness of the time. Verses 20–24, which report that the tree was withered up the next time Jesus and the disciples passed it, may have been added by a scribe with tendencies to either piety or tidiness. It is more likely, I think, that Jesus was pointing out the nearness of the end of all things.

As for the events of the last days and his crucifixion, Jesus saw these as the final intensification of the conflict produced by the Kingdom's arrival. The conflict itself is specified in the shouts of the crowds as Jesus entered Jerusalem riding on the colt of an ass: "Blessings on the coming kingdom of our father David!" (11:10) Then Jesus tells a parable that reveals something to the priests and lawyers of the city as well as to his disciples: it is the parable of the vineyard owner who sends his servants to reclaim his property and finally sends his own son, all of whom are peremptorily murdered by men in the vineyard. The priests and lawyers see that the parable is directed against them (12:12), and with increasing urgency try to think of a way to have Jesus arrested.

   After he has been captured, Jesus triggers his crucifixion by "admitting" he is the Messiah, the Anointed One. This, after months and months of secretiveness, when he has warned every-one not to reveal him! Obviously he had not wished the clamor resulting from popular recognition of his messiahship to interfere with his ministry before he was ready. Now the time had come, the Kingdom was at hand, and he was ready for the crucial battle.

   What did Jesus expect to happen after he was crucified? If we may rely upon the indications in Mark, he believed that he would be vindicated in his position as the Anointed One by being raised up. We have noted that in 9:9 he warned the disciples not to speak of the Transfiguration until after his resurrection. This is the first linking, in Mark, of apocalyptic thought with the Resurrection. Jesus' use of the title "Son of Man" in that context suggests the possibility of a reference to the teachings of the book of Daniel and to other apocalyptic writings in which the Messianic figure is somehow related to the resurrection and restoration of the Jews. Mark 10:32–34 says that Jesus, on the way to Jerusalem for the great events which awaited him there, told the disciples that he must die but that after three days he would be raised up. Again in that passage occurs a reference to the "Son of Man" title.

   Once again we must insist on looking at this matter through Jewish eyes contemporary with Jesus, so far as that is possible. In apocalyptic pattern, Jesus' death would be a high point in the struggle of the two ages, the one dying and the other being born. If and when God returned him from the grave, there would be an unmistakable sign of the Kingdom's having really arrived. Then the end of the world must come quickly, and the disciples, as arbiters of the Kingdom, would have even more power than they had displayed during the Messiah's earthly lifetime. Men would know, as Jesus reminded them from scripture in Mark 12:10–11, that the rejected stone had become the main cornerstone.

One curious text in Matthew's Gospel does not appear in Mark, but is so illustrative of Jewish apocalyptic expectations at this point that it should be alluded to. It is the brief passage in Matthew 27:51–53, when Jesus has just died, saying, "There was an earthquake, the rocks split and the graves opened, and many of God's saints were raised from sleep; and coming out of their graves after his resurrection they entered the Holy City, where many saw them" This text, which has been almost embarrassingly suprarational to many believers in modern times, may have simply described what most believers at that time *expected* to happen when Jesus was put to death. The New Order would begin to break out at once, and God's holy ones would be raised up to participate in it.

Now what, in terms of all this, did the word "salvation" mean in the ministry of Jesus? If we limit ourselves to the interpretation of this early gospel the answer should be rather obvious. Salvation, for Jesus, had to do with God's redemption of the whole Creation. An individual person was "saved" who had the secret of the Kingdom and was penitently waiting for its arrival. His salvation would be as total as that of Creation; that is, it would be both physical and spiritual. The very approach of the Kingdom was enough to bring healing and forgiveness to those who had faith or believed in its coming.

The word *soteria,* "salvation," and its derivative forms occur seldom in Mark. Two occasions when they do may be instructive. The first is when the rich ruler has gone away and Jesus has observed to the disciples that it is hard for such persons to enter the Kingdom. Immediately the disciples rejoin, "Who then can be saved?" (10:26) Salvation is obviously connected with getting into the Kingdom.

The second occasion is when Jesus is on the cross. Over his head is a placard which says "The King of the Jews," mocking his talk of a kingdom. Bystanders jeer. "He saved others, but he cannot save himself. Let the Messiah, the king of Israel, come down now from the cross" (15:31–32). The meaning is not quite so clear this time. Perhaps the reference was to Jesus healing and forgiving activities in general. But regardless of the specific implications, the verb "to save" is employed again with definite relationship to the claim of Jesus to be the Anointed One whose coming would usher in a new era.

Even though the Jewish Messiah viewed his work and ministry through the structures of apocalyptic thought, salvation was still, as in Old Testament days, related to the people of God and the land or the earth he had given them to occupy. It was not the isolated event in the life of a single individual which subsequent Christian history was to make of it.

### The Gospel for the Gentiles

It is evident from the second chapter of Acts that at least the earliest Christian preaching among the Jews followed the lines of apocalyptic thought we have been considering. Peter, the spokesman on that occasion, cited for the Jews gathered at Pentecost the prophecy of Joel about the Day of the Lord when portentous events would occur and God would pour out his Spirit on the sons and daughters of Israel. Then he said that he was speaking of "Jesus of Nazareth, a man singled out by God" (note that the emphasis is still on the *human being* whom God had called to messiahship), whom they, the Jews, had had killed by "heathen men" (the Romans). But God had raised Jesus from the dead, said Peter, fulfilling a prophecy of David in Psalm 16 that his soul would not be "abandoned to death." David's tomb being still in Jerusalem, it was evident that he was speaking of one yet to come, and that one was Jesus. "Let all Israel then accept as certain," said Peter, "that God has made this Jesus, whom you crucified, both Lord and Messiah" (2:36).

The Jews who heard this were touched to the heart and asked what they should do. "Repent," said Peter, "repent and be baptized, every one of you, in the name of Jesus the Messiah for the forgiveness of your sins; and you will receive the gift of the Holy Spirit. For the promise is to you, and to your children, and to all who are far away, everyone whom the Lord our God may call" (2:37–39). About three thousand persons, we are told, were baptized into the fellowship that day.

The miracles, the sense of awe, and their pooling of property into a common treasury all bespeak these early Christians' confidence that they were living in the last great upheaval of time, at the climax of which would occur the utter transformation of the earth. Apparently the impact of the witnesses to the Resurrection and the intensity of experiences such as the one at Pentecost sustained this confidence for months and even years.At least it is several years later, in the correspondence of Paul to the Corinthians and in the letter of an unknown writer to the Hebrews, for example, that we find witnesses to the gospel attempting to deal with the question of why the Messiah has not returned, finalizing, as it were, the Day of the Lord.

Meanwhile, the church faced a more immediate crisis. What should it do about Gentile men and women who were beginning to be attracted to the faith of the Christian Jews? Peter obviously had some problems about accepting the conversion of non-Israelites. Acts 10 records his dream about the "unclean" animals the Lord bids him eat, and his subsequent meeting with Cornelius, the centurion who has sent messengers to Joppa to urge him to visit Caesarea. Peter rehearses before Cornelius the salient factors of the Messiah's work in Israel: his death, his resurrection, and his command to the disciples "to proclaim him to the people, and affirm that he is the one who has been designated by God as judge of the living and the dead" (10:42). Then, we are told, the Holy Spirit came upon all those who listened. The Jews with Peter were astonished that this should happen to Gentiles. Peter asked if anyone could withhold the water of baptism from them, who had received the Holy Spirit just as the Jews at Pentecost had, and ordered their baptism in the name of Jesus the Messiah.

Paul's letter to the Galatians gives a less gallant picture of Peter's struggle with the Gentile question. There he recalls how he and Barnabas more or less "divided the territory" with Peter and James and John, agreeing that they themselves should go to the Gentiles and Peter, James, and John ("those reputed pillars of our society") to the Jews. When Peter came to Antioch, Paul says, he ate his meals with Gentile Christians. But then when "certain persons came from James" (apparently a Judaizing faction from Jerusalem) he withdrew from fellowship with these Gentiles, fearing the reproach of the Jews.

The question had to do with whether Gentiles must first become Jews, undergoing the rite of circumcision, before they could become Christians, or followers of the Jewish Messiah. Apparently most of those who had been associated with Jesus in his ministry insisted that they must, although Peter wavered at the boundary. Paul, who became the champion of Gentile Christianity, seems never to have been in great favor among the Christians at Jerusalem. Perhaps what the Judaizing Christians feared was that their gospel, originally couched in terms of Jewish apocalyptic expectations, would undergo serious or even fatal changes unless those who were baptized first underwent a significant transformation into the Jewish religion and life-style.

If they did indeed have such fears, these now appear to have been justified. Paul and other Christians who baptized the Gentiles into Jesus Christ without requiring that they first become Jews were so successful that within a few decades, or certainly within a few centuries, only minimal attention was paid to the fact that the gospel of the Messiah was even of Jewish origin, and while such teachings as the Day of the Lord and the Second Coming of the Messiah entered into the Gentile world, their substance was essentially altered by the cultural transposition.

The shadow of the problem surfaces in the famous 1 Corinthians 15 passage, which many New Testament scholars regard as the most important statement about the Resurrection in the scriptures. Paul was obviously answering a tendency among some of the Corinthian Christians to say that there is no resurrection of the dead. He argued that if that were true, then Christ was not raised, the gospel was untrue, and their faith was null and void. "If it is for this life only that Christ has given us hope," said the Apostle, "we of all men are most to be pitied" (15:19).

When we contrast this situation with the whole climate of Jewish apocalyptic, we see what a drastic change had already occurred. Here already was the notion of a fellowship of Christians with no expectation of a transfigured earth inaugurated by the resurrection of Jesus and accompanied by a general resurrection of the saints before it should be fulfilled. Clearly Paul felt the crisis for Christianity involved here. He struggled manfully to bring these Gentiles back into line with the Jewish philosophy of last things. Christ, he said, was raised from the dead as "the firstfruits of the harvest." As death had come by Adam (this alone indicates that the Gentiles had been trained in Jewish background), life would come through Jesus. Otherwise, asked Paul, why should some people seek baptism in behalf of those who are already dead? They hope to convert the dead, to make saints of them, to prepare them for the Day of the Lord when the saints shall be raised. Why, continued the Apostle, should some of us undergo such pain and effort to preach the gospel if we do not really expect things to be as we have said? It would be much easier to say, "Let us eat and drink, for tomorrow we die."

Next Paul dealt with a question on which there had apparently been much speculation, namely, what kind of body do the resurrected have? After talking of how seed is sown and grows into a different form, and how Christians die in one form and are raised in a spiritual form which defies further specification, he gave his summation, which is by this time partly Jewish, partly Greek in character:

What I mean, my brothers, is this: flesh and blood can never possess the kingdom of God, and the perishable cannot possess immortality. Listen! I will unfold a mystery: we shall not all die, but we shall all be changed in a flash, in the twinkling of an eye, at the last trumpet-call. For the trumpet will sound, and the dead will rise immortal, and we shall be changed. . . . And when our mortality has been clothed with immortality, then the saying of Scripture will come true: "Death is swallowed up; victory is won!" "O Death, where is your victory? O Death, where is your sting?" The sting of death is sin, and sin gains its power from the law; but, God be praised, he gives us the victory through our Lord Jesus Christ. (15:50–57)

The polemical situation in which Paul had to argue for the gospel over the years led him to expand greatly on the original features of Jewish apocalyptic. Contending for the acceptance of his central ideas, he was compelled to translate those ideas whenever possible into other cultural idioms. In what is considered his most formidable theological treatise, the epistle to the Romans, for example, he had to reckon with a strong sense of Roman legalism and individual responsibility. Therefore he talked at length about sin, grace, and righteousness, and assured the Romans that it is by dying into Christ or dying with him "in a death like his" that "we shall also be one with him in a resurrection like his" (6:5). The cultural preparation of these people for the gospel had not included Jewish apocalyptic; what had happened in Jesus had to be interpreted in a different fashion.

To Paul, the essential thing was to gather men into Christ, whether they understood precisely as Jews or not. He tried to educate them into Jewish ways of thinking, but he did not predicate the failure or success of his ministry on how well he accomplished that task. Whether his dedication to the Messiah eventually altered his own conception of salvation or not is a moot question, but at least his language, as he struggled to witness all around the Mediterranean, betrays strong evidences of what Martin Dibelius has called a "Christ-mysticism."[2] He was inordinately fond, says Dibelius, of the phrase "in Christ Jesus." Yet he did not use it of himself alone, but of all believers. Perhaps it had something to do with his loneliness as a Jew traveling extensively in non-Jewish lands: Christ became the mystical extension of all Jewry to him and the Christians in those lands. Bultmann suggests another reason for it: much of Paul's ministry was conducted among people who had been adherents of or were familiar with mystery religions in which union with the deity was the final object; it was therefore natural that he should seek to replace those deities in people's loyalties and affections withChrist, the judge of the living and the dead.[3]

In any event, we are beginning to become familiar with the problem of understanding salvation thought as it moved from one cultural situation into another. Whereas for Jesus and the disciples salvation was a matter of repentance and faith in the Kingdom which had long been promised and was breaking into their midst with imperative haste, for Gentiles who had not grown up with Jewish minds and expectations it tended more and more to be baptism into this mystical Christ, whose stature transcended that of a Nazarene whom God had elected to be the Messiah and became that of a deity who was himself empowered to be present in any place at will and behave as a Greek or Roman deity might. Certain features of apocalyptic thought might continue, such as the idea of a Day of Judgment and the teaching of a Second Coming, but less and less did they conjure up the body of Jewish thought from which they had sprung. The prophetic man who became the Jewish Messiah would come to be pictured as the Pantocrator Christ adorning the vaulted ceilings of Mediterranean basilicas, looking more otherworldly than the disciples probably ever expected.

# 2

# Twenty Innings and the Same Ball Game?

My preacher by the fountain square never tired of saying that he had no creed but the Bible. He was proud to belong to a tradition that boasted of having no tradition. "Back to the New Testament" was almost a watchword with him. He didn't have much truck, as they say, with anything that smacked of popery or institutionalism. He was free to interpret the scriptures for himself. Nothing stood between him and Jesus.

I can still appreciate how he felt. It felt good to me, too. "Nothing between," we used to sing, "my soul and the Savior."

But I have since come to realize that there is much between. About twenty centuries, to be exact. Twenty centuries of human development. Twenty centuries of changing culture. Twenty centuries of interpretation. And there may even have been a new ball game in the *first* century!

I'm not knocking the mystical thing—feeling the presence of Jesus and all that. I have my own moments. But twenty centuries of changing human life are bound to have produced some major dislocations in the line of our theological transmission. It is impossible today to speak with complete authority about almost any-

**25**

thing Jesus did or said. It is all subject to two or more interpretations.

As I said, my preacher read history, but not Church history. If he had read Church history—really read it, not just looked at the names and dates—he would have been a lot less sure of some things. Like his ability to understand the exact meaning of everything Jesus said. And his own freedom from tradition.

The only way to break away from our own captivity, of course, is to try to get some perspective on matters. That means a kind of historical overview. We can't do much in a mere chapter—maybe skip a pebble across the surface and linger a moment wherever it touches down. But that will at least suggest the important interrelatedness of soteriology—the study of salvation—and the political and social aspects of the Church's long existence.

## The Deification of the Messiah

I noted in the previous chapter how the transition of the gospel from Jewish culture into the Hellenistic world was a critical passage in which increasing emphasis was placed on the idea of being "in Christ." For four centuries to come, the question of the nature of Christ was to be the fiercest battleground for theological debate within the Church itself.

One of the most prevalent philosophies or theologies in the entire Greco-Roman world was the one known as Gnosticism. There were many varieties of this position, both within and outside the Church. In general, they all held that man's salvation is through a certain *gnosis* or knowledge, a kind of mystical supernatural wisdom enabling him to transcend the evil world of matter. They seemed to stem, on one hand, from Platonism, the Greek idea that the physical world is only an imperfect embodiment of the more real world of ideas known to the mind, and on the other hand from the ancient Persian dualism which saw good and evil as engaged in continual combat in the world.

One reason for Gnosticism's popularity was its highly syncretis-
tic character. It did not hesitate to adapt to whatever form of
religious belief or practice it encountered, thus in effect conquer-
ing by joining it. Nor did it hesitate to join Christianity. The apocalyptic flavor of early Christianity, its expectation of the end of a
corrupt world, its talk of the righteousness of God, its emphasis
on the morality of its followers—all these things made it especially
congenial to the Gnostic's general frame of reference. Therefore
Gnosticism and Christianity became entangled in the churches as
early as the first half of the second century.

Perhaps the most important thing to understand is the effect
Gnostic philosophy had on Christianity's understanding of its
Messiah. Because to the Gnostic mind all matter is inherently evil,
Gnostic Christianity insisted from the first that Christ only *appeared* to be fleshly but was in fact a spiritual being masquerading
as a man. The God of whom Christ spoke, said the true Gnostic,
was not the same God of whom the Old Testament spoke, for he
was a much higher, more spiritual being. The God of the Old
Testament was only some kind of demiurge, an emanation of the
true God. For this reason Marcion, one of the most powerful of
Gnostic thinkers, insisted on excluding the Old Testament from
use in the Church.

In the light of this important struggle in the early Church to
define its beliefs or doctrines, it is perhaps easier to see why these
beliefs were formulated as they were. Gnosticism finally lost the
battle, but not without exacting certain compromises from the
Christian theologians.

The Church retained its belief in the manhood of Christ. The
doctrine of the Incarnation, in fact, became one of the central
tenets of its faith. Christ became flesh and dwelled among us. This
rescued the Jewish notion of the essential goodness of matter and
the created order. But, on the other side of the question, the
Church largely forgot the earliest idea of the Messiah's being a

man with a totally human background, who was then anointed by the Spirit of God to be the long-expected Son of Man. More and more stress was laid upon stories of a miraculous conception and of a strange, inexplicable combination of divinity and humanity in the person of Christ.

When Christianity finally became a legalized religion under the emperor Constantine early in the fourth century, it held a "world-wide" council in Nicaea to determine what its orthodox teachings were. To appreciate the theology of the Nicene Creed we must remember that the Church had been growing in a variety of different climates and cultures for nearly three hundred years. The men who gathered in Nicaea to hammer out some consensus for the faith came as representatives of widely divergent viewpoints. The documents they fashioned were as much the result of political compromise as any conciliar papers arranged at a modern bargaining table. If they contained truth, it was truth by compromise, not truth by the sudden intervention of God.

What the Council of Nicaea declared, as the climax of all the Church's quarrels over Gnosticism and Arianism and other theological persuasions, was that Christ was actually begotten of the Father in heaven and was of "the same essence as the Father." In other words, the final seal was given to the kind of compromise that was being worked out as early as the end of the first century when the Fourth Gospel was written. Jesus was miraculously fathered by God in an otherwise human birth. He dwelt in the flesh, experienced the pains of the flesh, ate when he was hungry, died a real death, and was buried in a tomb. But at the same time he was divine, consisting of the same substance as the Father, and remained above human sin. He was the God-Man, "very God" and "very man."

Without pressing the matter further, it is possible to observe how far such an emphasis was from the Jewish beginnings we noted in the Gospel of Mark. There Jesus was seen to be the

Messianic figure whose presence heralded the breaking in of the New Age in which the earth would be transformed. While he was obviously an important figure because of what he was the key to, he was actually subordinate to the arrival of the Kingdom which God was engineering. At Nicaea, Jesus himself was made divine and given a status equal to that of the Almighty. Salvation became more and more the property of a centralized Church with a unified doctrine.

Do we need to point to the effects in our own time of the great creedal compromises of the early Church? Think of the millions of Christians who stand in their individual churches and recite the words, "I believe in God the Father Almighty, maker of heaven and earth, and in Jesus Christ his only Son, our Lord, who was conceived of the Holy Ghost, born of the Virgin Mary, suffered under Pontius Pilate, was crucified, dead, and buried. . . ." Is it any wonder their minds boggle at the contradictions they are asked to believe? Would it be helpful to them to know that the very first Christians probably made no such attempt to hold the humanity and divinity of Christ together because they had no need to do so?

## The Church as the Custodian of Grace

The more the Church developed as a social and political power in the Middle Ages, the more it saw the desirability of controlling not only the doctrines men believed but the access they had to salvation. In the beginning, the desire for centrality and order among believers was probably for the believers' own welfare. Ignatius' words to the Trallians, early in the second century, have a benefactory tone: "When you are submissive to the bishop as to Jesus Christ, it is clear to me that you are not living as ordinary men but according to Jesus Christ, who died for us that you might escape death through faith in his death." By the time of Irenaeus at the end of the same century, the tone is firmer: "The faithful everywhere must needs agree with the church at Rome; for in her the apostolic tradition has ever been preserved by the faithful from all parts of the world." Origen, fifty years later, would say, "Outside the Church, no one is saved."

The means of salvation that the Church increasingly accentuated during these early centuries was the sacrifice or substitutional death and atonement of Christ. Obviously this was an early development in the Church's life and thought: it is certainly present in Paul's theology and in New Testament literature generally. But the relationship between Jesus's crucifixion and the slaughtering of the Passover lamb seems not to have been part of the very earliest stage of Messianic thought. It probably developed a little later, when the Church began to become conscious of itself as the New Israel and—extending the analogy—regarded the slain Messiah as the sacrificial animal connected with the escape from bondage. It is even possible that Jesus himself initiated such a connection during his Last Supper with the disciples, although it is unlikely that he would have pressed it if he anticipated resurrection and the immediate inauguration of the New Age.

The point is, the Church legitimately picked up the substitutional atonement aspect of Jesus's work and gradually gave it more emphasis until it overshadowed all other aspects. And this, as the Eucharist or Communion came increasingly to be identified as the repetition of Christ's atoning death, centralized access to salvation in the priesthood of the Church. As Cyprian, bishop of Carthage in A.D., 248–258, said,

> If Christ Jesus, our Lord and God, is himself the high priest of God the Father, and first offered himself as a sacrifice to the Father, and commanded this to be done in remembrance of himself, then assuredly the priest acts truly in Christ's stead, when he reproduces what Christ did, and he then offers a true and complete sacrifice to God the Father, if he begins to offer as he sees Christ himself has offered.

By the early fifth century, Augustine's famous book *The City of God* developed the idea that there are two cities growing together in the world. One is the City of God, to which belong all those who are Christ's and confess to being strangers and pilgrims on the earth. The other is the Earthly City, symbolized by Babylon and Rome. All citizens, including Christians, said Augustine, should live obediently in the Earthly City, preserving order and decency. But that city will eventually pass away, and the City of God will go on forever. Then those who are in Christ will reign with him.

"Therefore the church even now is the kingdom of Christ," said Augustine, "and the kingdom of heaven. Accordingly, even now His saints reign with Him, though otherwise than as they shall reign hereafter; and yet, though the tares grow in the church along with the wheat, they do not reign with Him."

In the medieval Church, then, the Church and the Kingdom were regarded as one and the same, although it was recognized that there might be some in the Church who were there under pretension and would not be saved.

Augustine also put great emphasis on the validity of the Church's sacraments regardless of the character of the priest administering them and even of the attitude of the person receiving them. Pelagius, a monk from the British Isles who had won a wide reputation and settled in Rome, taught the essential freedom of the individual will. Augustine, in a great controversy with this man and a follower named Celestius, insisted instead on the absolute sovereignty of the will of God, which must obviously rule out the possibility of free will in men.

As a part of the thinking that insisted on human determinism, Augustine propounded the doctrine that the sacraments of the Church are valid *ex opere operato*—that is, regardless of the will of those who participate in them. Suppose a priest is a profligate and immoral person. Is the Communion he serves a true sacrament? Yes, answered this teaching of Augustine. Suppose a man takes Communion under false pretenses. Is it also valid then? Here the answer was somewhat equivocal. It was valid for the man if he was repentant at the time; but, even if he was unrepentant, the sacrament was still potentially valid.

This is all very complicated, but it illustrates how strong a grip the medieval Church was attaining in the matter of salvation. By controlling the sacrament of baptism, it controlled the means of entering the Church. By controlling the sacrament of Communion, it controlled the continuing mediation of Christ's atoning death. By the high Middle Ages, the Church could even force kings and emperors to do its bidding by threatening to withhold salvation from them and their subjects. In one dramatic case in 1077, involving Henry IV of Germany and Pope Gregory VII, the rebellious Henry was finally released from the pope's excommunication only after appearing barefoot in the January snow on three successive days outside the castle where the pope was residing.

The sacramental system grew more and more fixed during the Middle Ages until by the thirteenth century seven sacraments of the Church were recognized as being, in Augustine's words, "visible signs of an invisible grace." These were: baptism, confirmation, communion, confession, penance, marriage, ordination, and extreme unction. Through these major rites, the Church exercised enormous control over the life of every individual who belonged to it. A person was baptized as an infant and received catechetical instruction in order to be confirmed at puberty. All his life he required Communion in order to appropriate the sacrifice of Christ for his sins. But before he could take Communion, he must confess his sins to the priest, be absolved for his good intentions, and perform whatever act of penance the priest assigned. If he married, the Church must bless the union; if he did not, and went into Holy Orders, the Church must administer ordination. Finally the Church must minister to him at death, preparing him to meet God in the Judgment.

The man of the Middle Ages had few questions about the nature of salvation. It was otherworldly in its emphasis and clear in its manner of attainment. Its object was to prepare men for the great Judgment scene in the heavens, where Christ was pictured as a stern and implacable jurist who could not be deceived. He had given the keys of his Kingdom to representatives on earth, however, and whatever was transacted by them here would be sealed by him there. The man who wished to escape the fires of hell and dwell in eternal bliss had merely to humble himself before the pope and his priestly servants, receive the sacraments of the Church from them, and pray to be received into the everlasting Kingdom.

Lest we become too easily critical of such a system, we should bear in mind how fundamental to human nature is the desire for such a definite method of achieving salvation. Portestantism too has produced its systems of doctrines or teachings with adherents who insist that salvation is to be had only within them. Lutherans, Presbyterians, Baptists, and others, like the Roman Catholics, have been prone to assert that they alone have found the way to the Kingdom.

**The Break in the System**

There were many attempts through the centuries to correct abuses in the Church's system. The names of Bernard of Clairvaux, Wyclif, Hus, and Savonarola are instantly associated with various efforts at reform. So are the names of Francis and Dominic, who founded the famous orders of mendicant friars. These preaching friars quickly spread throughout western Europe, revitalizing the Church as a popular force among the nations. None of these figures, however, actually conceived of breaking away from the Church at Rome and establishing a new communion. They only sought to make the system itself more responsive to certain kinds of needs.

Nor did the great Reformation movement of the sixteenth century, which eventuated in a real schism in the Church, begin with the intention of breaking away from Rome. Luther, who inaugurated the events that led to the rupture, was to describe himself as a man climbing a bell tower in the middle of the night who, when he slipped and fell, grabbed at the rope and woke the whole populace.

It began over the sacrament of penance. Throughout the later Middle Ages, popes had resorted to the selling of indulgences in order to raise funds to support their work. These were paper documents granting purchasers absolution from sin. A pardoner, or person licensed to travel and sell indulgences, supposedly sold the papers to contrite persons in lieu of other acts of penance.

Such a method was obviously open to abuse. In Luther's Germany, this seemed to arise from the fact that Pope Leo X was desperately trying to raise money to complete the majestic basilica of St. Peter's in Rome. He had commissioned a Dominican named John Tetzel to make the collections for indulgences in the area where Luther lived. Apparently there was considerable feeling among the people about Tetzel's approach—a feeling not unrelated to patriotic hesitation to see all this money flowing out of Germany. Tetzel, moreover, made the most extravagant claims as to the benefits to be had from his indulgences.

Luther had been involved in constant anguish for several years over the question of his soul's salvation, and had been teaching biblical studies during that time on the books of Psalms, Romans, Galatians, and Hebrews. He had become convinced that salvation is a matter of personal faith and commitment, not something the Church can effect by mere sacraments. When Tetzel came along, therefore, Luther preached against the abuse of indulgences, and on October 31, 1517, posted on the door of the castle church in Wittenberg (which was commonly used as a bulletin board for the university), his famous 95 theses.

No one would have guessed that they were so revolutionary as to produce the reaction that followed. They did not deny the pope's right to sell indulgences, but merely questioned the extension of indulgences to souls in purgatory and other matters related to the abuse of the system. The theses were intended, moreover, for academic debate—not as the match to ignite a prairire fire. But Tetzel and others took them seriously and started a major campaign against Luther. One thing led to another, and soon the formidable monk was writing broadside after broadside against the entire sacramental system.

This is not the place to go into the larger history of the Reformation, which may be got from any competent writer on the subject. What we need to examine is rather the effect produced by Luther, Calvin, Zwingli, and other reformers on the way men of their time came to regard salvation. In major outline, the changes brought about by the reformers were:

a renewed emphasis on salvation by grace through the faith of the individual in the promises of God;

renewed interest in the scriptures as the source of our knowledge of the ways of God and of how salvation is brought to men;

a new emphasis on hearing and understanding the Word of God;

a repudiation of earthly hierarchies between the individual and God; and

a reduction in the number of sacraments, and a rejection of their "magical" character.

The overall effect of the Reformation on salvation thought was a strong new accent on the individual or personal dimension. The biblical notion of the "priesthood of all believers" became extremely important. This is why the preaching and hearing of the Word were restored to centrality in the reformers' churches, while sacramentalism assumed a more minor role; faith was to arise from the encounter between the individual and the preached or written Word. There was a flurry of translation activity as scholars sought to make the scriptures available in the vernacular languages. Luther and Calvin began an energetic tradition of producing commentaries on the Bible. Schools and universities were founded for the training of a literate ministry, competent in the scriptures. Among the so-called "radical" reformers, including Thomas Müntzer, emphasis was placed on the Holy Spirit and his leadership of the individual Christian. Even among Lutherans, Calvinists, and Zwinglians, where more attention was accorded the scriptures, the guidance of the Spirit in interpretation was extolled.

Almost from the beginning of the Reformation, Protestant groups began to speak meaningfully of "the New Israel," reviving the self-conception held by the early Church that it was to receive the fulfillment of the promises made to the ancient Jews. Calvin, Knox, and others attempted to establish theocratic communities in which they controlled the political and spiritual government. The founding fathers of New England apparently regarded the American experiment in similar terms, for their government was controlled by the Church, they often called their territory "New Canaan," and the Hebrew language was at one time proposed as the official language of the wilderness colonies. In this sense at least there was a renewal of the Old Testament accent on "a people and a land," although it coexisted with the well-entrenched tradition of looking for a City "not made with hands."

Despite the emphasis on individual faith, however, there continued to be instances of severe repression of thought and practice in the churches and sects of the time. Luther finally consented to the decimation of radical groups and Calvin's memory is besmirched by the infamous trial and execution of the Spanish theologian Servetus, who opposed him in Geneva. The history of religious intolerance in almost every country of Western Europe is an unpleasant one, and the narratives of oppression in America, the home of religious asylum and freedom, are at times nearly incredible. Regardless of how strongly men protest that they believe in individual conscience and personal faith, there is something in most of us that appears to fear differences or resistance to conformity.

## Modern Religion as a Personal Business

Two major factors in the thinking of the Reformation have continued to exert significant influence on the history of redemptive thought. One is the growing emphasis on human understanding represented by the philosopher Erasmus and other humanists, and obliquely reflected in the reformers' belief in men's ability to respond to the "reasoning" of God with them about their salvation. We shall have occasion to examine this factor at more length presently.

The other factor is the constant insistence on individual responsibility in the soul's relationship to God. Luther's own progress toward belief in the individual priesthood of the believer was marked by a strong sense of the importance of personal experience. He was a mystic by nature and carried over a mystical tendency from Roman Catholicism into his teaching of the soul's union with God through Jesus Christ. In all the Protestant churches, and especially among the radical sectarians, experientialism became an important test of religious belief.

This emphasis on experience was to lead to consequences of unusual proportions in the development of the pietistic and evangelical movements in Europe, Great Britain, and America. In America, for example, the entire revivalist pattern from Edwards and Whitefield in the eighteenth century to the work of Billy Graham and Oral Roberts in our own time depends heavily on the doctrine that salvation is by grace through faith—that it can occur instantly in the sinner's life and is often accompanied by strange movings of the Spirit and unusual feelings in the person being saved.

Because the first great revival in the colonies, known as the Great Awakening, broke out along the seaboard and then became the principal style-setter for frontier religion as it crossed the continent, American religious thought has been more singularly stamped by a strong individualistic pattern than that of any other Western nation. Pioneer minds, already highly individualistic, insisted on independence in spiritual as well as political matters.

Doctrinal differences were innumerable and led to splinterings and schisms and the formation of new sects and denominations. Yet there was consensus on two things: a man's religion was a matter primarily between him and God, and it manifested itself in his behavior in the community. However mutually exclusive or contradictory these two ideas may appear, they were not thought to be so among zealous churchmen and sectarians.

There has been so much uniformity in our attention to the evangelistic pattern, in fact, that cynical voices have often mentioned what might be called the "revivalistic stereotype" operative in American religion generally. When Professor William G. McLoughlin, Jr. wrote a history of revivalism from Charles G. Finney to Billy Graham,[1] he was quick to observe that the only real development from Finney's time to Graham's has been in terms of method or technique for conducting meetings—not in terms of the theology or message of the evangelists. Indeed, McLoughlin points out that revival sermons tend to be shallow and full of clichés about being lost and then found, convicted of sin and then repenting, trusting God for his grace and believing in the Lord Jesus Christ for his atonement; and that they also abound in contradictions about how free and unmerited salvation is, yet what man must do in order to be saved.

1. *Modern Revivalism* (New York: Ronald Press Co., 1959).

Despite the general emphasis on personal faith, there is a division of feeling among Americans on the question of revivals and evangelistic preachers. Some people feel that "old time religious meetings" are the touchstone of religious fidelity, and they measure the worth of a particular church or way of worship against the overtly experiential cast of such meetings. Others express the fear that the pitch of emotionalism often reached in such meetings is merely the product of excessive evangelistic methods and not of the Holy Spirit, and that they are manufactured or "whipped up" by skillful crowd manipulators in order to take advantage of people. The revivals of recent years have had their share of detractors on this very point, and the Graham team has been especially vulnerable because of the high degree of sheer mechanical skill displayed. A typical word of criticism is that voiced by the editors of the *Christian Century* magazine in 1957: "Our objections are to the Graham procedure which does its mechanical best to "succeed" whether or not the Holy Spirit is in attendance. At this strange new juncture of Madison Avenue and the Bible Belt the Holy Spirit is not overworked; he is overlooked.[2] Revivalism in the Graham meetings, said the editorial, is "trumped up"; it is "manufactured kairos."

Graham, like other revivalists in American history, has strongly emphasized the instantaneous character of salvation. At various times he has assured radio and television audiences that they could be saved "at this very moment" in their automobiles, by their television sets, or even sitting in a bar or tavern. Oral Roberts, who combines evangelism and faith healing, invites people to kneel down where they are, place their hands on the radio or television set, and receive the Holy Ghost to make them whole.

The same evangelical emphasis which has informed American revivalism and popular religion has shaped numerous "witness-

2. Cited ibid., p. 513.

ing" groups such as Youth for Christ, Campus Crusade, Lay Witness, Lay Renewal, and the current Jesus Movement. Among these groups, as among certain fundamentalist or sectarian church organizations, the approach to salvation tends to be extremely simplified.

The person offering his witness is likely to begin by asking the person witnessed to if he is a Christian or if he has been saved. If the answer is no, the person witnessing may then begin to quote selected verses of scripture which constitute, for him, the way of salvation. A widely used pattern is to start with Romans 3:23, which says categorically that all men are sinners, proceed to Romans 6:23, which says the wages of sin are death but the gift of God is eternal life through Jesus Christ, and then bring the presentation to a climax with John 3:16, John 3:36, John 5:24, or some other text indicating the need of the individual to believe in Jesus, repent of his sin, and give himself into God's hands.

I do not wish to call into question the testimony of persons whose experience of redemption has proceeded from some sudden conversion or illumination produced by the methods I have just described. That is not at issue here. But it ought to be pointed out that cultural developments since New Testament times have put considerable distance between early and later meanings of the terms employed.

Obviously the modern evangelical witness, even if it speaks of entering the Kingdom of God, does not understand precisely the same thing by Kingdom of God as the Jewish disciples of Jesus did. The present understanding has been conditioned to mean something far more otherworldly than the scriptures themselves indicate. Even among the Children of God, one of the groups in the contemporary Jesus Movement emphasizing the imminent end of all things, the Kingdom is synonymous with heaven and implies escape from the present situation.

The current emphasis, moreover, is much more privatistic than that of Jesus and the Apostles. True, it speaks of love and brotherhood. But it conceives of salvation as an experience which happens to a person in his inner being, in his aloneness, in his isolation from the world and other persons. The ancient Jew, with his sense of the individual's reliance on the community for his larger being and his belief that the promises of God were to a nation of people and not to individuals alone, could probably not have understood such a gospel.

The so-called social gospel movement in this country a few decades ago may have helped some persons to recapture part of the communal dimension of Christianity. It insisted that the Church has not heard the gospel if it has not acted to clothe the naked, feed the hungry, and minister to the outcast. Yet even this movement was far from being identical with the vision of which Christ spoke, of a transcendent Kingdom crashing in upon the present order like the briny spray of a rising riptide breaking across the rocky shoreline.

## The Necessity of Going On

This has admittedly been a very sketchy picture of soteriological patterns through the ages. But it does provide some orientation as to the way salvation thought has shifted according to various changes in the cultural and societal environment. The reader who has had little or no introduction to such a picture before may well feel bewildered by this time, as if someone had been at work moving all his old familiar landmarks. I sympathize with him, for I too have experienced the pain of disillusionment. I still do, for that matter. We probably never get beyond feelings of disappointment at having lost trust either in persons or ideas that were once dear to us. Yet it is part of growing up and learning to test things for ourselves.

Learning to forgive is also part of growing up. Grudges are luxuries only the very young can afford. Even grudges against oneself. We must accept our pasts, even if they were wrong or naïve, because they are our pasts. They belong to us. They are part of what we are today. To hate them, to disown them, is to hate and disown ourselves.

I have forgiven my preacher by the fountain square for not having told me these things. He probably never knew them. Or if he did, he was profoundly disturbed by them. They would have made his work so much less clear. And besides, I cherish the bittersweet memories of my evangelical youth. As long as the fountain square was the unchallenged linchpin of the world, the umbilical center of the universe, that simple plan of salvation seemed adequate to all my needs.

Now, of course, is another matter. Not for me only, but for most of us. My children don't even have a fountain square. Television ended the fountain square business forever. And my oldest son, who is still in grade school, has already lived in five cities, including a year abroad when he was in the first grade and had his European history classes in the Louvre. As Wolfe said, you can't go home again. Not any more.

But what sense are we to make of the salvation thing? Must we give it up, now that we see how relativized it has always been? Can we give it up?

No, we can't give it up. We aren't made so that we can. It is into us too deep. Centuries and centuries of yearning for it, praying for it, working for it, cannot be thrown over just like that. It has shaped us in such a way that we shall always be inclined toward it, even if we live a hundred lifetimes.

Some persons think they have given it up, when all they have really done is to change the name tag on it. Our modern secularized world is literally brimming with surrogate salvations—education, scientism, psychoanalysis, physical culture, philanthropy, black magic, group therapy. You name it, and we're trying it. We can't get over our deep-seated urge to find personal fulfillment and to save the world. Nearly everyone you meet or read about today has some need or scheme to save society. Presidents, monarchs, captains of industry, scientists, doctors, teachers, chambers of commerce, even hippies and Yippies—they all want to do something to improve mankind.

The result is that most of us live with a kind of subconsciously amalgamated notion of what salvation is and what will save the world. I say subconsciously because we rarely objectify this urge to be saved or identify it in any integral way with the salvation the Church has always talked about. We simply move along from day to day with a blurred sense of the relationship between the two, assuming it is good to work for an improved world, but never asking specifically what the notion of progress in the milieu has to do with Jesus Christ and the kind of personal salvation evangelists and the Church are always talking about.

Most preachers are not very helpful either, for they too are unsure about what the relationship is. They feel an obligation to talk about Jesus and to preach sermons based on biblical texts; yet at the same time most of them sense the tremendous cultural gulf between New Testament times and our own, and proceed rather uncertainly to discuss matters of social and ethical conscience which spring directly from the context of today's world. Conservative laymen in most churches insist that they hear enough about the world from their newspapers and television sets, and come to church to hear about things of the spirit. And statistical reports show that the congregations that thrive the most phenomenally are those that are most antiworldly and fundamentalist in their beliefs. The minister who does plunge right in and try to clarify the relationship of personal faith to secular modes of redemption is actually releasing his own constituency to work out their salvation in the world at large and to reduce their dependency on him and the institution that pays his salary. This discourages many clergymen from following through even on their own curiosity as to the relationship.

Where does that leave us? Quite alone with our questions, in most cases. Pilgrimages are necessarily lonely things. If they weren't, they wouldn't be pilgrimages.

But we must go on, however hard the way. We cannot go back to the fountain square, once we have learned it is not the center of all that is. Even if we shut our eyes and pretend with all our might, we can't go back. It is never the same any more. And we cannot simply rest in our confusion. We may be confused, but we are never content to be. Nor are we made to be nonreligious. Sometimes, repudiating the religions of our childhood, we affect a blasé attitude toward religion. But it doesn't really satisfy us, for it goes against an inward yearning to believe something and believe it so strongly that it reorients our personalities and christens them with power. We have to go on. However difficult or painful, it is the only way.

I hope the following chapters do not contribute to the difficulty. They are meant to alleviate it. In them, I have tried to flush out into the open the sense of reverence our society in general and some of us in particular have for a few of the surrogate salvations I spoke of. In most cases, my own reverence for them will be apparent too. But I have tried also to be critical of them and to ask, "Is this another fountain square?" For we mustn't merely trade one set of idolatries for another, which is what we frequently do in our attempts to get away from where we are and arrive somewhere else.

Once we have looked squarely at some of these modes which hold so much redemptive hope for contemporary man, and have confessed that they are part of our hidden agenda of anticipation too, we should be in a better position to answer the question that really has to be asked, namely, "What does all this have to do with my religious belief? How is it related to Jesus and the salvation of man?'' If we can answer that with any degree of satisfaction, we will be on the road to wholeness as persons of the modern world. And Christian persons, at that.

# 3

# Salvation and the Little Red Schoolhouse

One of the conditions that made the Protestant Reformation possible was the tremendous revival of learning in the fourteenth and fifteenth centuries. One thing led to another. The recovery of classic languages led to new interest in ancient manuscripts. Interest in the manuscripts led to the restudy of biblical texts. The restudy of biblical texts led to the new doctrinal positions of Luther, Zwingli, and Calvin.

But the Reformation was only a by-product of the renascence of learning; the renascence continued to cut its own wide, deep channel. In 1592, only seventy-five years after Luther tacked his theses to the church door, the Englishman Francis Bacon declared that he had taken "all knowledge" to be his province. "The mind is the man," he said, "and knowledge mind; a man is but what he knoweth."

Bacon drew up his plans for a *Magna Instauratio,* a Great Reconstruction of philosophy and science unparallelled in history since the time of Aristotle. He would lay the foundations for a whole new empirical science whereby man could eventually discover and occupy all the distant continents of knowledge and power. Bacon was convinced that knowledge is power, he was laboring, he said, "to lay the foundation not of any sect or doctrine, but of utility and power."

Knowledge did become power, even to Bacon. A relatively poor man with lavish tastes, he was arrested for debt in 1598. Yet his varied abilities and comprehensive knowledge made him too valuable to leave languishing in prison. Released, he was appointed to one important committee after another, and rose to great prominence in the government. In 1606 he was made Solicitor General; in 1613 he became Attorney General; and in 1618 he was awarded the high office of Lord Chancellor.

The zest for *scientia* or knowledge has continued unabated ever since. At times it has existed side by side with religious intent, as in the humanism of Erasmus, More, and Colet in the sixteenth century, in the founding of colleges and universities such as Harvard, Yale, and Princeton for the training of ministers, and in the devotional attitudes of such great intellects of the recent past as Teilhard de Chardin and Paul Tillich. Jonathan Edwards, the famous fire-and-brimstone preacher of eighteenth-century New England, wrote an impressive scientific essay on spiders as a boy of twelve, graduated from Yale at seventeen, and is still regarded as one of the outstanding philosophers of his age. At other times the quest for knowledge has appeared essentially divorced from theological considerations. Locke's famous *Essay on Human Understanding* in 1689 declared that the mind of man is at birth a *tabula rasa,* a blank tablet, and that all knowledge is derived subsequently from experience and the senses. Such a declaration, powerfully argued, was bound eventually to undercut the old idea of divine revelation. By the nineteenth century, major philosophers in every Western country were in basic agreement that the salvation of man lay principally in his learning to use his rational powers to decipher the code of the universe and fashion a better life. In the words of Nietzsche, "Not mankind but superman is the goal."

### The Arrival of "Information Environment"

It was inevitable, given the development of technological aids for recognizing, retaining, and recalling data, that the accumulation of information should become enormous. Marvelous as the human brain is, it has not proven capable of assimilating and correlating an almost infinite number of chunks, large and small, of raw knowledge. The computer, on the other hand, is an excellent device for this purpose. If designed with enough sophistication, it can perform almost limitless tasks of storage, recall, and correlation.

On the positive side, this "information environment," as McLuhan calls it, provides a measure of control over natural situations which man has never had before. Computerized medical service is an illustration. It is expected that all medical knowledge will one day be coordinated through vast computer systems in one or two locations in the world. Computers programed to "examine" ailing patients will record information on pulse, temperature, respiration, reflex ability, skin condition, chemical analysis, and so on. These computers will then "consult" with the data bank in the computer center, and the center will issue a complete statement on the patient's physical situation, including a prescription for treatment. Doctors will devote their time essentially to medical research and to adding information to the data bank. Every patient will be assured of the most accurate diagnosis of his condition possible at the existing stage of medical science.

Similar storage and coordination of data will be possible in other areas of human research as well. Some scientists theorize that information banks, which can be reduced to microscopic size, will someday circle the globe in satellites in order to facilitate telecommunication. It is even conjectured that console data-receivers will be available for use in the home, very much as television receiver sets are used now. Instant access to worldwide information, music, and literature will be a feature of daily life for man in the twenty-first century.

Not even Francis Bacon could have foreseen such fantastic possibilities!

But there are negative aspects as well.

Bacon was right when he said that knowledge is power. Those who control the information environment control the people who live in that environment too. By deciding which information to program and how to arrange its programing, they determine the values of various kinds of information. And, as Ivan Illich complains in *Deschooling Society,* valued information becomes a kind of currency. Nations barter with it. The people who have it become a new aristocracy. Those who don't cannot compete.

The rearrangement of international power patterns according to information hoard is already becoming apparent. It appeared publicly in the old joke about the Russians and Americans after World War II, in which both sides claimed, "Our Germans are better than your Germans!" Power shifts and alignments have been made ever since on the basis of who had the information to build a nuclear bomb or interplanetary rockets or ICBM's. Now the data battle has obviously moved beyond weaponry to such matters as agriculture, economics, and communication. Nations without the old-fashioned wealth to purchase scientific equipment and the brains to operate it are finding themselves even further behind in the race for the new kind of wealth. Emerging nations and perennially destitute ones are at the mercy of data-rich countries which dangle handouts in front of them in exchange for vital natural resources.

Within countries, similar rearrangements of power occur according to the same principle. Emerging technocrats quickly parlay data combinations into vast corporate holdings and political influence. Even persons who have belonged to the old aristocracy of wealth, power, and influence find themselves suddenly dependent on the new informationists.

At this point the contest appears to be the old familiar one we have been through thousands of times in the history of man, only with a new set of face cards. Maybe it is the same old contest. But it becomes much more frightening than before when we realize how exponentially swift the build-up of data-control is. It was one thing to reach the juncture in history when one nation could field an army with gunpowder against another nation's army of lancers and bowmen. But we are at the state when scientists are on the track of modifying the DNA molecules that determine human personality. George Orwell's famous antiutopian novel *1984* may turn out to have been a rather accurate timetable after all. Suppose we are on the brink of an era when genetic control actually comes within the reach of man. Hitler's dreams of a superrace will no longer seem such fantasies. And what distortions of humanitarian ideals will the power of that single set of data produce? There may be something salutary about knowledge; but it also contains the seeds of destruction.

At yet another level, there is a second problem attached to informational accumulation. Many critics are saying that the presence of such enormous stockpiles of data is finally dehumanizing to man. Because he cannot absorb the knowledge in existence, it assumes a kind of facticity over against him and begins to threaten him. That is, all the data become *things* crowding his world. He becomes aware of knowledge pollution and feels depressed about it. After all, he cannot destroy knowledge; it keeps reproducing its own kind, like some hideous parasitic fungus choking and clogging the life pores.

Karl Marx observed that the industiral revolution separated man from his work. Now, says Ivan Illich, the knowledge revolution has separated man from his learning. What a man learns, that is, is principally what he is given to learn. He gets it by rote, is stamped with diplomas and degrees certifying his "worth" in society, and carries what he has learned as a commodity wherever he goes. The thrill of discovering what one knows, of being intimately involved with it, has largely been lost in our culture. Beckett's *Godot* satirizes the way we carry around learning that is not truly ours. As Didi and Gogo wait by their leafless tree, they meet a stuffy old character named Pozzo and his unfortunate beastlike servant named Lucky. Lucky is the walking repository of countless words, phrases, and syllables from man's philosophical past, and he recites them at the drop of a hat. Here is the main example we are given in the play:

Given the existence as uttered forth in the public works of Puncher and Wattmann of a personal God quaquaquaqua with white beard quaquaquaqua outside time without extension who from the heights of divine apathia divine athambia divine aphasia loves us dearly with some exceptions for reasons unknown but time will tell and suffers like the divine Miranda with those who for reasons unknown but time will tell are plunged in torment plunged in fire whose fire flames if that continues and who can doubt it will fire the firmament that is to say blast hell to heaven so blue still and calm so calm with a calm which even though intermittent is better than nothing but not so fast and considering what is more that as a result of the labors left unfinished crowned by the Acacacacademy of Anthropopopometry of Essy-in-Possy of Testew and Cunard it is established beyond all doubt all other doubt than that which clings to the labors of men that as a result of the labors unfinished of Testew and Cunard it is established as hereinafter but not so fast for reasons unknown that as a result of the public works. . . .[1]

Lucky's speech is about four times this length, but this sample is sufficient to indicate its nature. Scholars will puzzle for years over the allusions in this passage. As a friend and protégée of James Joyce, Beckett can be expected to telescope numerous references into single phrases or even syllables. But here he has tellingly

1. Samuel Beckett, *Waiting for Godot* (New York: Grove Press, 1954), p. 28.

demonstrated the foolishness and the obvious burden of man's carrying around thousands of ill-digested ideas and sayings which are but the accumulated mental junk of many generations of philosophers and teachers.

Yet another absurd dramatist, Eugene Ionesco, has built an entire play around the foolishness of pedantry and the way we permit our lives to be victimized by it. *The Lesson* takes us into the study of an enormously erudite pedagogue and lets us behold the unscrupulous way he uses his meaningless knowledge as power over a young girl who has come to him for her weekly instruction. Here is an example of the gobbledygook he purveys.

> That which distinguishes the neo-Spanish languages from each other and their idioms from the other linguistic groups, such as the group of languages called Austrian and neo-Austrian or Hapsburgian, as well as the Esperanto, Helvetian, Monacan, Swiss, Andorran, Basque, and jai alai groups, and also the groups of diplomatic and technical languages—that which distinguishes them, I repeat, is their striking resemblance which makes it so hard to distinguish them from each other—I'm speaking of the neo-Spanish languages which one is able to distinguish from each other, however, only thanks to their distincitve characteristics, absolutely indisputable proofs of their extraordinary resemblance, which renders indisputable their common origin, and which, at the same time, differentiates them profoundly—through the continuation of the distinctive traits which I've just cited.[2]

Whenever the girl attempts to challenge something he says, the professor reminds her of his superior knowledge, cites some equally ridiculous bit of information, and proceeds with the "Lesson."

The entire drama becomes an extended illustration of Illich's remarks in an article for the *Saturday Review:* "The more learning

2. Eugene Ionesco, *Four Plays,* trans. Donald M. Allen (New York: Grove Press, 1958), p. 61.

an individual consumes, the more 'knowledge stock' he acquires. The hidden curriculum therefore defines a new class structure for society within which the large consumers of knowledge—those who have acquired large quantities of knowledge stock—enjoy special privileges, high income, and access to the more powerful tools of production."[3] By "hidden curriculum," Illich means "the framework of the system" itself, the previously determined scale of values attached to various pieces of information. Because this framework is settled on the individual from above, he is obligated to learn things that are of little purpose in his life except as commodities to be bartered for income and position.

The knowledge game is played with different denominations of currency in many settings besides schools and laboratories. Businessmen are familiar with the way it is played in courtrooms, insurance companies, and sales offices. Doctors and nurses know how it is played in hospitals and medical centers. Churchmen even play it in churches, where other kinds of knowledge are sometimes deprecated in favor of biblical or theological knowledge, or where direct revelation or knowledge of *God* is a kind of supertrump.

It is obvious that those who control the knowledge banks enjoy a superiority over those who lack control. What may not be quite so apparent is that the data themselves often exert invisible control over the person or persons possessing them. Often they determine how a person will respond to particular stimuli, delimiting his freedom in ways of which he is not even conscious.

### The Problem of Knowledge Fatigue

We don't require the *reductio ad absurdum* of Beckett or Ionesco to realize the extent to which many persons today feel over-

3. Ivan Illich, "The Alternative to Schooling," *Saturday Review,* June 19. 1971, p. 45.

whelmed by the sheer abundance of information. Something plainly happens to the emotional state of persons who experience informational overload. Students who were eager to acquire knowledge in the early grades become increasingly apathetic as they discern how absolutely limitless the horizons of knowledge are. Many psychologists believe that the huge dropout phenomenon in secondary schools and universities is partially attributable to widespread depression over the impossibility of mastering all there is to know.

I recall a conversation with a young woman who tried to commit suicide while in graduate school. An honor student in high school and college, she had become greatly interested in history and had been appointed student assistant to her major professor during her last year of college. She was excited by her work when she arrived at graduate school and spent long hours in the library reading and preparing her assignments.

"While I was doing research for my thesis," she said, "I spent hours and hours a day in the library. I became more and more conscious of how much information was in the books on those shelves. Some days I couldn't work because I was so much aware of all the information. I even began to imagine that the books were talking. They would all talk at once, so that you couldn't understand anything."

Finally, after weeks of despair, she took an overdose of pills. Someone discovered what she had done, called an ambulance, and she was rushed to the emergency room of a hospital where her stomach was pumped and her life was saved. But she had no desire to live, and said she might try it again someday.

The young lady was clearly a victim of information overload. Confronted by all there is to know in the mastery of a single field today, she lost her will to achieve. It seemed to her, as it does to many other students, that there was no virgin territory left. Every subject had already been exhaustively researched and documented. She could turn nowhere in the world of information without feeling that many feet had trod the ground before hers.

We can only wonder how many such victims of the information environment we come in contact with each day. Housewives feel bombarded by all kinds of information on which products to buy for the home, how to care for the skin and hair, which foods to feed their families, what chloresterol-producing substances to avoid, how to rear children, how to remain alluring, and on and on; it comes in the mailbox, it is broadcast on TV and radio, it is handed to her by the salesman at the door, and it is passed on by energetic well-wishers at every social gathering she attends. Professional workers must annually contend with tons of pamphlets, books, advertisements, and even filmstrips, all crammed with information about earning a living, preparing for the future, keeping stock up to date, maintaining low overhead, getting sufficient mileage, using proper stationery, fighting unfair taxation, avoiding legal entanglements, keeping abreast of the field, reading the right newspapers, supporting the best legislation, and taking the most relaxing vacations.

Sometimes the United States Postal Service and the communications media seem to be engaged in a gigantic conspiracy to bury the average consumer under an ever-expanding pyramid of nonessential information and advice. Countless sober and serious persons want to tear out their phones and TV's, paint over their mailing addresses, and shut off the channels between themselves and the outside world; or else escape to some beautiful Shangra-La where the world is once more comparatively innocent of knowledge, where knowledge fatigue and information overload are virtually unknown, and where human beings seem to have the edge on the discovery and accumulation of factual data.

It is a serious problem. In the medical field alone, a practicing physician who does not read at least one good medical journal regularly and return to medical school for refresher courses once every five years is considered by his more aggressive colleagues to be grossly negligent in his responsibility for his patients and for the field of medicine itself. More development in medical science occurs every ten years now than occurred in the entire history of man from the beginning to 1950.

Surely the question all this raises about the relationship between salvation and knowledge is obvious. If man is to be saved by what he knows, *which* knowledge is important? Who is to say, in all the rapidly expanding fields of data-gathering, which pieces of information contribute to the wholeness or redemption of man and which do not? No one is really capable of embracing all knowledge today. Systems spin off new systems and galaxies new galaxies.

Man must become the "hunter," says McLuhan. He must determine which myth he wishes to build into the information environment, and then hunt the pieces he needs to confirm the image he envisions. The environment is so vast and so crammed with information that it is possible to construct almost any myth and sustain it.

Does this mean there is no one pattern, no one template, according to which man should understand his salvation? Is he the arbiter of his own fate, so to speak—the captain of his own destiny? Is he justified in fashioning whatever myth or myths seem good and proper to him at the time, and then, if he changes his mind, in destroying them to erect new ones?

The Zen Buddhist might say he is. Zen views man as an extremely finite creature who lives in a great void. Most of his life he is victimized by illusions of one kind or another. Salvation to the Zen is enlightenment, or *satori,* which is a kind of seeing to the secret of the way things are, so that one does not struggle against them any more. When one does not struggle and is relaxed, nothing hurts him. He finds joy even in the experiences of hurt, suffering, and the void. Consciousness itself becomes a source of joy.

Perhaps one of the reasons for the apparent allure of Zen for university students in this country over the past ten years has been its laughing defiance of the information environment. Students have had their circuits blown by the overload of knowledge, and Zen has said, "Feel the void, it is good." Drugs have been another way of taking the same trip; they have helped young people to exist in the face of the knowledge explosion.

We should be sober about the place of knowledge in our lives. It *has* improved the quality of life in many instances. Few of us would want to revert to earlier cultures in which disease and death were more rampant than they are now and life was generally less predictable. But there is something dehumanizing about information too plentiful to be appropriated by the individual. "Is this what life is for?" we ask. It almost makes us want to become know-nothings, to turn our backs on the astronomical compilation of data and become primitives again.

## Education as Ecstasy

There are more optimistic voices, however, saying that the information environment can be a positive force for life. It need not be a tyrannous surrounding, they say. Man has only to adapt to a new consciousness in which he allows data machines to do the laborious part of knowledge gathering and storage. He himself is then free to enjoy the fruits of such an environment.

According to this way of thinking, the whole world is on the verge of the possibility of a "liberal education." For decades the term has been questioned. It refers to the educational ideal of the ancient Greek city-states, when only the free man (liberated, liberal) was given training for the liberal arts. Slaves had other things to do. In our own country it was John Dewey, the father of progressive education, who said that a liberal education for all men is ridiculous in a society comprised primarily of workers. Dewey put an emphasis on practical or functional learning.

But now cybernetics promises to give all workers more and more freedom. The forty-hour week, which was once a seventy-hour week, is already giving way in many places to the thirty-five- and thirty-hour week. "People complain that technology is dehumanizing," say the proponents of the cybernetic approach. "That is foolish. Technology actually makes it possible for us to be *more* human. By reducing the number of hours we must spend in monotonous, repetitive jobs, it gives us the time required to engage in the arts, recreation, and various forms of sociability."

There is a new strain of educators who advocate a freer, more selective approach to learning. They admit that some people must master certain specialties in order to make the new society function; but even these persons, they maintain, need not sacrifice their entire being to their specialties; they can keep a great portion of themselves for investment in other things.

"Let's learn a few 'how-to' things to make the new society functional," say these educators. "But then let's keep our perspective on living by enjoying those parts of the environment that excite us and help us to grow as persons."

George B. Leonard has written a book that has already become something of a classic along this line. It is called *Education and Ecstasy.*[4] Leonard's contention is that education has been boring to students because of its heavy traditional orientation and repetitive methods. Most children could easily acquire the foundations of learning in less than a third of the time presently allotted to them, he says. What we must do is purge ourselves of dedication to areas of subject-matter which derive from earlier ages without relevance to our own; we must also abandon our laborious methods of imparting information. Echoing Dewey, but with both feet

4. New York: Dell Publishing Co., 1968.

planted in the technological age, Leonard insists that education should be "a new apprenticeship for living," appropriate for life in the future.

Alvin Toffler follows the same argument in *Future Shock.* Why should all students, regardless of ability or preference, be compelled to study mathematics, grammar, and science? Why shouldn't a new curriculum be oriented around other subjects, such as the periods of human life, the process of social relationships, or the understanding of human sexuality? With the development of recent sciences, these latter topics are of far more immediate worth to most people than the former. Why should they be given only slighting attention in the schools?

We ought, says Toffler, to be giving children Ray Bradbury to read instead of Shakespeare. Not that science fiction is nobler and better styled than the classics of our mother tongue. But it teaches readers to deal imaginatively with the problems of the present and the future instead of orienting them toward the past.

In this view, which is being adopted by free schools in many parts of the country today, the child or person being educated is regarded with utmost respect for his individuality. There is no preconceived mold into which he must fit. He is not thought of as an empty tin into which ideas and information are to be funneled at gross rates measurable by standard quizzes and exams.

Man is basically inquisitive, say the proponents of this approach. He wants to learn. It is only when he is restrained from following his own interests and told "You must learn this" or "You must remember this" that he begins to balk or withdraw. If permitted to retain his inner-directedness, he not only learns much more swiftly but ventures into far more territories of learning.

Leonard is unqualified in his statement of expectations: "What we fail to acknowledge is that every child starts out as an Archimedes, a Handel, a Nietzsche."

It is possible that Leonard had in mind some words of R. Buckminster Fuller, the inventor of the geodesic dome and one of the world's most celebrated thinkers. Fuller is universally regarded as a genius. Yet he said a few years ago:

> I am convinced that neither I nor any other human, past or present, was or is a genius. I am convinced that what I have, every physically normal child also has at birth. We could, of course, hypothesize that all babies are born geniuses and get swiftly degeniused. Unfavorable circumstances, shortsightedness, frayed nervous systems, and ignorantly articulated love and fear of elders tend to shut off many of the child's brain capability valves. I was lucky in avoiding too many disconnects.[5]

Even those who argue for the traditional system of educating the young find it difficult to controvert the idea that most human beings accomplish far more by inner motivation than by compulsion. An educator in a free school in New York related the story of a mother who came to the school to check on her child's progress. When she visited the child's class, she found all the children engaged at various games. Her own child was playing Monopoly. Furious at this costly waste of time, the mother stormed into the director's office. The director suggested that she return to the room and join in the game for a few minutes to see what the children were "learning." When she did, and was given a turn at rolling the dice and moving her token on the board, she counted off the requisite number of places. "Oh no, Mama," her child admonished, "we're playing in base-four!"

### The Schoolroom of the Future

Even a progressive school such as the one just mentioned seems old-fashioned in comparison with the version of a school of A.D. 2001 depicted in the final chapters of Leonard's *Education and*

5. From "Education for the World of 1984 and 2000," in J. A. Battle and Robert L. Shannon, eds., *The New Idea in Education* (New York: Harper & Row, 1968), p. 106.

*Ecstasy.* Leonard hypothesizes a visit to a fully automated school environment of the next century. Children are not compelled to attend school any longer. It is simply so inviting and exciting that they go because they want to. There are no formal hours or regular classes. Instead there are interest centers and equipment environments. Children progress at their own speeds and according to their own inclinations.

Basic educational tools are acquired through computerized machines. The children find it difficult to believe that their parents spent twelve years acquiring the basics they themselves learn in a few months, and that their parents found school boring.

Teachers are present not as regulators but as senior partners. They share their own educational development with the children as the latter seek such sharing. They are, so to speak, experienced persons in residence.

Nor is learning confined to the school grounds. The entire human environment has become a learning environment. Businesses, corporations, and institutions have discovered that they exist primarily to provide educational opportunities for people. The family unit is conceived of as a matrix for growth and development. Every facet of existence in the modern city and world community is regarded as part of a unified network of learning opportunities. Education is the primary business of human life.

The ecstasy to which Leonard alludes in the title of his book and of which he speaks at length is simply the constant delight experienced by persons who are interacting with the information environment and being changed by it.

If education in the coming age is to be, not just a part of life, but the main purpose of life, then education's purpose will, at last, be viewed as central. What, then, is the purpose, the goal of education? A large part of the answer may well be what men of this civilization have longest feared and most desired: *the achievement of moments of ecstasy.* Not fun, not simply pleasure as in the equation of Bentham and Mill, not the libido pleasure of Freud, but ecstasy, *ananda,* the ultimate delight.

Western civilization, for well-known historical reasons, has traditionally eschewed ecstasy as a threat to goal-oriented control of men, matter and energy—and has suffered massive human unhappiness. Other, civilizations, notably that of India, have turned their best energies toward the attainment of ecstasy, while negelecting practical goals—and have suffered massive human unhappiness. Now modern science and technology seem to be preparing a situation where the successful control of practical matters and the attainment of ecstasy can safely coexist; where each reinforces the other; and, quite possibly, where neither can long exist *without* the other. Abundance and population control already are logically and technologically feasible. At the same time, cybernation, pervasive and instantaneous communication and other feedback devices of increasing speed, range and sensitivity extend and enhance man's sensory apparatus, multiplying the possibilities for understanding and ecstasy as well as for misunderstanding and destruction. The times demand that we choose delight.[6]

The essence of such an educational goal lies in man's submission to change as he confronts the environment. "To learn is to change," says Leonard. "Education is a process that changes the learner."

It is in this profoundly simple and simply profound supposition that this version of education differs so radically from most traditional views. Traditional learning had to do mainly with the preservation of culture. Information and attitudes were passed on from generation to generation in such a way as to preserve the continuity of the present with the past. The new view assumes the continuity, but glorifies the future more than the past. It is far more interested in discovery than in the preservation of former ways of life.

6. Leonard *op. cit.,* p. 17.

### Is Change Itself a Form of Salvation?

Among those who speak positively for the value of change as a life-principle, one who has a unique qualification is George Gallup. As a poll-master by profession, Gallup has long been concerned with the dynamics of human change and how it is engineered by those desiring it. In a book called *The Miracle Ahead,* he speaks of the natural conservative tendencies in any population, and how these tendencies inhibit progress in human institutions. "In the whole history of man," he says, "no genera-tion has been taught to expect change, to be prepared for change, or to seek change."[7]

Yet, as Toffler has so well reminded us, ours is a time of un-precedented change in almost every area of life. Change is occur-ring at dazzling speed. A Rip Van Winkle who fell asleep for twenty years today would be astonished indeed when he awoke; the interval would seem more like a century or two.

What shall we do in the face of change? Is anything to be gained by trying to flee or putting our heads in the sand like the ostrich? What we really need to do, says Gallup, is to educate people to the dynamics of change and its significance. One of the most cogent reasons for learning to cope with it is that persons properly oriented toward change enjoy better mental health. Studies by psychologists of the victims of disaster in World War II indicate that people survived difficulties better if they accepted what was happening to them without living in constant protest against it.

The population says Gallup, must not only come to an apprecia-tion of the role of change in their lives; they must learn to demand change of their leaders.

The peroration of Gallup's book is a ringing assertion of

7. This and following references to *The Miracle Ahead* are from Battle and Shannon, eds., op. cit., p. 173.

his belief in man. It is almost incredibly unqualified in its optimism.

Can man perform the miracle of lifting himself to a higher level of civilization?

The answer is Yes—unequivocally. Man is clearly in charge of his own evolution; he can proceed at a pace that he himself sets.

He can solve any problem that comes within his purview—even the problem of war. The great advances made in physical science can be paralleled in social science. Man now has the procedures for dealing with the problems arising out of his social existence—problems that the methods of physical science cannot adequately explore or illuminate.

Man has scarcely begun to make use of his almost limitless brain power, either individually or collectively. Lack of progress in dealing with the affairs of mankind can be traced to a simple truth; man has never made a concerted and persistent effort to solve his social and political problems. His inventive genius has been confined almost exclusively to the production of better tools and instruments.

The next great move forward can now be taken. All that is required is a firm belief in man's great potentialities and a readiness to accept change.

Man is still young on the face of the earth; civilization is still in its infancy. *Homo sapiens* has not yet realized his strength and his greatness; nor does he see, except dimly, the heights to which civilization can reach.

Three hundred years ago it was equally difficult to foresee the great advances in science that the future held in store. Only Francis Bacon had that vision. He also had a vision of man with which this book might properly close: "Men are not animals erect but immortal gods."[8]

8. Ibid., p. 176.

Somehow we cannot forbear asking whether this is not merely a gratuitous restatement of the old salvation-by-progress doctrine which has emerged again and again in man's history. Is it predicated too naïvely on Herbert Spencer's notion that everything in the world evolves into ever better forms? Does it overlook the possibility that evil as well as good is inherent in education and change? We tend to sympathize with Leonard's ecstatic view of the educational process. But something inside us catches at Gallup's bold assertion of man's apotheosis, his becoming godlike. We remember Buchenwald and Auschwitz, which were also the products of a "super" race.

**This Is Where We Came In**

Some of us have the feeling that we have been through all this before. We remember the utopian dreams of the nineteenth century, the talk of a Golden Age, and glorious theories about human perfectibility, the power of reason, and the basic goodness of man. We also remember World War I and the pessimism that settled over such talk.

On the theological scene, disillusionment with the idea of progress produced the monumental careers of Karl Barth and Reinhold Niebuhr. Barth did not talk about men's being "immortal gods" instead of "animals erect"; he sounded instead a note of diastasis, and said that there is an infinite qualitative distance between God and man. Human reason, he declared, can never reveal the presence of God to man; only God can reveal himself. We have vastly underestimated the power of evil in the world, said Niebuhr. It is everywhere. It infests our human institutions. We must quit pretending it does not exist and face the realities of political life in the world. Neither the atheistic rationalist nor the committed Christian is going to win any triumphant victory over the forces of evil. We must settle instead for compromises and proximate wins, and content ourselves with devising strategies for partial good.

The famous words of St. Paul, "The good which I want to do, I fail to do; but what I do is the wrong which is against my will" (Rom. 7:19), might well have been the motto of neoorthodoxy in the years between the two world wars.

Most of us are basically optimistic about education. Perhaps it is only a myth, but we generally believe that education does improve persons, particularly if it is a vehicle of moral values. The entire public school concept in this country is founded on such a belief.

But the question of moral values cannot be dismissed easily. Values are conveyed by educational systems even when we are unaware of it or try to exclude them from consideration. They were very much in evidence in the grammar schools of Puritan New England, where even the primers studied by boys and girls learning to read and write contained maxims inteded to edify their souls. Now, in schools where an attempt is constantly made to eliminate sectarian views, the value system is not clearly spelled out. Nevertheless, it is there. It is there in the kinds of stories and poems children read, in the songs they sing, in the social sciences they are taught, in the attitude imparted to them about the earth they live on.

Who monitors this subliminal indoctrination? No one, really. Most of it proceeds out of traditions from the past, or out of the biases of teachers and writers of textbooks and schoolmasters and colleges of education. Occasionally someone raises a cry about an idea that is being purveyed by a particular approach or textbook being used. Blacks have exerted considerable pressure in recent years to rectify the educational implications of materials based on centuries of social injustice. But for the most part there is no authority scrutinizing either teaching methods or teaching materials for the consistency or philosophy of values being imparted to schoolchildren during some of the most formative years of their lives.

I am not advocating that any board or agency be authorized to conduct such a scrutiny. In the final analysis, the anarchy of values in public education may be the best course for avoiding the tyranny of a single viewpoint or system.

But the medium is the message, as McLuhan has so forcefully reminded us, and even the advanced educational system envisioned by George Leonard imparts significant moral values to those who train in it. The question is, what are those values and do they lead to the redemption of human life? Or is the only value in such a progressive system change for the sake of change, a joyride with many turns in the road but no ultimate destination?

It may be answered, of course, that Man is the destination. Without knowing that that is what he is really about, the student who is free to follow his own interests and inclinations must come at last to some crystallization of his personhood—to the end result of all his vagaries and studies. For, to be sure, Bacon was not entirely wrong in saying that man is what he knows. We are, approximately at least, the sum total of what our genes and experiences have made of us.

And to satisfy the orthodox religious mind we have but to recall that Jesus' favorite self-appellation in the Gospels was Son of Man, *barnasha,* which more literally meant simply Man. Paul calls him the second Adam. He was Man as God intended Adam to be. And in some sense, when we become Man through the educational process, we have an inner identification with archetypal Man.

But the quarrel over whether man is innately good or innately evil will not easily be put down. If he is indeed good in himself, then bringing out the self through education may eventually prove redemptive. If, however, he is evil or falls prey to evil when he does not mean to, there is no guarantee that the best educational process conceivable will lead us to a state of salvation. The Man produced by Leonard's version of the educational environment may be the first Adam, not the second; and the fatal tree in the midst of Paradise was the tree of the knowledge of good and evil.

# 4

# Saints in an Air-Conditioned, Lint-Free Universe

It has been nearly a quarter of a century since Fred Brown wrote his short story about an electronic superbrain, but two lines in it continue to be remembered around the world.

"Is there a God?" the machine was asked.

"There is now," it replied.

Henry Adams, scion of the famous American family, guessed the future of the machine when he attended the Great Exposition in Paris at the end of the nineteenth century. Crowds of people surged upon the exhibit of the great dynamo and gaped as if it were something otherworldly. Adams also visited Chartres, the medieval town some fifty miles from Paris, and walked through the famous cathedral with the most beautiful windows in the world. He noted that there were not many people there. They were all in Paris, worshiping at the throne of the dynamo.

Something seems to happen to human consciousness in a technological setting. It has become a cliché that God hardly seems necessary any longer. Michael Polanyi, the eminent philosopher of science, says that most people worship only a "God of the gaps" anyway. Anything they can't explain or do by human reason or human engineering is the mysterious province of the deity.

As the gaps in our knowledge and scientific feats are closed, his province necessarily shrinks.

Eventually, it is supposed, there will be no gaps. Or at least they will be microscopic. Then what of God? He will have been squeezed out of existence, as in Huxley's *Brave New World*. Technetronics and wonder drugs will have taken his place.

As Arthur Clarke (the renowned expert on space who wrote *2001: A Space Odyssey*) says, Fred Brown's words about the super computer are "more than a brilliant myth"; they are "an echo from the future." Theologians, says Clarke, have made "a slight but understandable error—which, among other things, makes totally irrelevant the recent debates about the death of God. It may be that our role on this planet is not to worship God —but to create him."

## The Switchover to Spaceship Earth

Clarke's words may ring in our ears as blasphemy. But there is no denying that the shift from an agrarian culture to an industrial and then an electronic culture has resulted in some important changes in the human psyche.

The manner in which we conceive of God is derived fundamentally from an agricultural stage in human development. Our inspirational literature tends even today to connect him with rustling trees, expanses of desert, rolling oceans, and so on. Yet millions of persons now spend their lives in air-conditioned houses and office buildings, shuttling from one to the other in high-powered automobiles driven along treeless plains of cement. Can they honestly and fully worship a God conceived in the language and images of a culture stage they have never really known?

Paul Tillich said in *The Future of Religions* that the spiritual consequences of living in the technological era cannot be separated from the emotional consequences. We no longer *think* the way men used to think. Maybe we no longer think the way *we* used to think.

Historians of culture talk about the revolution in human thought that occurred when Copernicus and Galileo produced in our midst the awareness that the earth is not the zero-center of the universe. Tillich saw the beginning of space travel as a radicalization of that revolution.

One of the results of the flight into space and the possibility of looking down at the earth is a kind of estrangement between man and earth, an "objectification" of the earth for man, the depriving "her" of her "motherly" character, her power of giving birth, of nourishing, of embracing, of keeping for herself, of calling back to herself. She becomes a large, material body to be looked at and considered as totally calculable. The process of demythologizing the earth which started with the early philosophers and was continued ever since in the Western world has been radicalized as never before. It is too early to realize fully the spiritual consequences of this step.[1]

In Freudian terms, man's extraterrestrial explorations have finalized his leaving the womb. He is like a child who has begun to leave home, to spend the night away, to dream of being on his own. In some ways, he will always take his mother's God with him; in other ways, he will feel that he has left that God behind.

The thousands of people who gathered on the Sheep Meadow in Central Park to watch the first moon landing on a giant screen, and the millions more who sat awe-filled in front of television sets, were passing through the shock of a cultural transformation whether they knew it or not. Something clicked in their minds. The earth was no longer the mysterious mother: it had become a planet to subdue. A reverence slipped away, unnoticed. The word "earth" no longer had the old quality about it. It had become

---

1. Paul Tillich, *The Future of Religions* (New York: Harper & Row, 1966); cited in *Contemporary Religious Issues,* ed. Donald E. Hartsock (Belmont, Calif,: Wadsworth Publishing Co., 1968), p. 355.

equivalent to "planet." It was somehow smaller, more comprehensible. It could be rationally conceptualized, held at arm's length like a tennis ball, and subjected to planning.

It was no accident that the first popular mobilization of concern about the ecosystem and what man was doing to it followed directly upon the heels of the manned space shots. It may be surmised that this was the moment when we first realized with unmistakable clarity that the earth was finite and destructible, and that its Creator might not lift a little finger to save it. The earth is man's, and the fullness—or emptiness—thereof.

We now see with a kind of apocalyptic terror the collision course we were on. The prophets of ecological crisis in our midst sound like the old biblical voices of doomsday. "We must repent," they scream through all the media, "or we will all likewise perish." The crisis bell is ringing on what Buckminster Fuller calls Spaceship Earth. All hands are at work to avert disaster.

Technology has been in some sense the villain. Actually it is neutral, of course, and may be used either beneficially or otherwise. In our ignorance we have used it otherwise. The science of cybernetics, using computers to monitor and redesign computer service, was applied to industrial production in such a way as to increase it tremendously. GNP and GWP shot up fantastically. But the earth was not unlimited in its resources. We could not ravage it on one hand, grubbing raw materials for our factories, and poison it on the other, dumping sewage and unrefinable wastes into the water and pumping noxious gases into the air, without quickly producing a critical situation.

One of the most impressive reports on the biosphere yet seen is by the so-called Club of Rome, entitled *The Limits to Growth*. Compiled by a seventeen-member team from MIT, the report is based on a systems dynamics approach to computer modeling which made possible a study of the complex interrelationships among five principal world variables: population, food supply, natural resources, industrial production, and pollution.

"If the present growth trends in world population, industrialization, pollution, food production, and resource depletion continue unchanged," concludes the team analyzing the data, "the limits to growth on this planet will be reached sometime within the next 100 years. The most probable result will be a rather sudden and uncontrollable decline in both population and industry capacity."

Loren Eiseley has caught this helter-skelter lunge for destruction in the image of a man on a commuter train. Eiseley boarded a train in New York. It was midnight and he was glad to be getting out of the city. As he entered the smoking compartment, he noticed a gaunt man in shabby clothes sitting with a sack in his lap. His head was thrown back and his eyes were closed. Eiseley supposed he was drowsing, either from exhaustion or from liquor.

As the train threaded its way out of the city and hurtled along the tracks, the conductor came through the car calling for tickets. Everyone, fancied Eiseley, was watching the derelict.

Slowly the man opened his eyes. He fumbled in his pocket and produced a roll of bills. "Give me," he said in a deathlike croak, "—give me a ticket to wherever it is."

The conductor held the roll of bills, stupefied. He rambled over the list of stations. The man's eyes were closed again and he did not answer. Finally the conductor extracted the price of a ticket to Philadelphia, thrust the bills back into the man's hand, and departed. People returned to their papers.

"In a single sentence," says Eiseley, "that cadaverous individual had epitomized modern time as opposed to Christian time and in the same breath had pronounced the destination of the modern world. One of the most articulate philosophers of the twentieth century, Henri Bergson, has dwelt upon life's indeterminacy, the fact that it seizes upon the immobile, animates, organizes, and hurls it forward into time. In a single poignant expression this shabby creature on a midnight express train had personalized the terror of an open-ended universe."

Eiseley studied his own ticket as the train sped on. It no longer seemed to be what he had thought it was. As he left the train, he stared again at the man. Was the sack full of money, he wondered, and had the man been riding thus a hundred years, the way a star might wander for ages on the highroads of the night?[2]

Perhaps the aimlessness is over. Now we see the planet more clearly as planet. It has certain dimensions, certain resources, certain capacities, certain possibilities. Plans are afoot to correct the steerage and establish the new society. Government committees are beginning to study the feasibility of world ordinances regarding the major variables of earthly existence. Some nations have already reached or are approaching ZPG—Zero Population Growth. Deadly emissions from automobile engines have already been cut back to levels of a decade ago. Scientists are tripling research programs to develop the use of solar energy. Architects are bringing domed cities with oxygen and heat control closer and closer to reality. Electronic capabilities for telecommunication and the computerization of both information and structural services are already far beyond the average citizen's imagination.

The spaceship may be saved. But what of life aboard?

## Changing Sensibilities

There can be no doubt that the technetronic era is fundamentally altering human sensibilities. As McLuhan said in *Understanding Media,* "The effects of technology do not occur at the level of opinions or concepts, but alter sense ratios or patterns of perception steadily and without any resistance." We are changed so silently and subtly as to be unaware of what is happening.

Other technological innovations in earlier eras doubtless produced similar alterations. Fire, the lever, the wheel, dynamite, the

2. Loren Eiseley, from a university address printed in J. A. Battle and Robert L. Shannon, eds., *The New Idea in Education* (New York: Harper & Row, 1968), pp. 46–47.

printing press, the steam engine, television, atomic fission—each has created a new situation, a new milieu, a new ball game for mankind. And no one has ever been exempt from the changes made in the society around him.

An attempt to opt out of the new milieu can be seen in the Amish people of this country. For years the fathers of Amish communities forbade concessions to the modern way of life. There are still Amish families who dress entirely in black and wear clothes joined together with pins instead of buttons. But evidence of the gradual breakdown of even this strong-willed, honorable old way of life may be read in the large automobiles driven by some of the prosperous, more liberal Amish men in place of the black buggies carrying their conservative relatives, which still ply along the modern highways. The chrome on the automobiles is painted black as a concession to the old ways. But change is inevitable in such a situation.

"There is no escape from convenience," says William Rodgers,

whether it is desired or not. For the very forces which produce and promote the products and gadgets of convenience mandate the withdrawal of alternatives, enforcing changes in a way of life whether or not those whose lives are changed welcome, ignore, or fight it. What was once a luxury, as in the case of electricity, the telephone, and the automobile, becomes essential to daily life and mobility. When suburban sidewalks and bicycle paths were obliterated and public transportation either diminished or did not expand, ownership of an automobile became less a matter of choice than a matter of mobility essential to employment.[3]

Most people in a society are relatively unreflective and will not hesitate to adapt to technological changes which appear to provide added convenience to their life-styles. The usual pattern is for the affluent to lead the way, then for others to follow. Television

3. William Rodgers, *Think: A Biography of the Watsons and IBM* (New York: New American Library, 1969), p. 301.

sets, for example, were once a novelty to be found primarily in bars, hotel lobbies, and the homes of the rich. Now the skyline over ghetto areas of every major city from San Juan to Singapore is crisscrossed by TV antennas.

This is why George Leonard says that "revolution by technology is far more effective than by ideology or violence."[4] It so thoroughly pervades a culture, modifying its life-styles, that it inevitably affects everyone, even those opposed to it. There is little point in looking back to the "good old days" of forty years ago, or in attempting to resist the pressures of the times to sweep us into the current of burgeoning technologies. None of us is able to remain inviolate. The changes in culture touch us all.

## The Threat of Dehumanization

The very fact that technological revolution is inevitable probably contributes to one of the chief protests lodged against it, namely, that it is dehumanizing. It does not wait for individual consent, but invades the culture on all fronts, suborning the individual's will before he has an opportunity to decide whether he wants it or not.

As Jacques Ellul complains in *The Technological Society,* machines at first appear to be the servants of man but eventually become his master. Since they have a basically more rational character than man, their efficiency gain is consistent. Becoming more and more sophisticated, they reduce man to a greater and greater dependency. In the end, he is little more than a piece of machinery himself, a cog in an interrevolving series of wheels.

The humanistic tradition itself becomes a luxury or an indulgence. Scholars in American universities who compete for government aids to research are well aware that federal programs are already heavily slanted toward scientific projects. Those who design the spending of public monies seem to know without con-

4. *Education and Ecstasy* (New York: Dell Publishing Co., 1968), p. 95.

ducting any polls or consulting any oracles that investigations of celestial gravity factors, oceanic sonar vibrations, and parabolic humidity control are far and away more vital than research projects concerned with aesthetic or philosophical matters.

I vividly recall participating in a year-long discussion group between American and French Protestants in Paris. The subject for the monthly conversations was Anglo-French relations. On the French side, discussants became most animated (one man was almost violent) when attention was turned to the so-called "Americanization" of western Europe. "You are ruining all our traditions," they said. "Your corporations have come into our countries and industrialized them. Now technology is eroding everything we held dear about our lands and peoples."

What these persons, mostly businessmen themselves, failed to see is that Americans are not the villains. America herself is being victimized by the technological revolution. Perhaps one reason the revolution succeeded so well here is that we had so little tradition to oppose it, by comparison with European countries whose humanistic roots are so deep and venerable. But the technetronic era is no respecter of nations. It will eventually dominate the globe. Whether the supercomputer is god or not, it will be omnipresent.

William Rodgers recounts in his biography of the Watsons and IBM a moment in the history of the company whose initials have become synonymous with corporate, computerized existence, when someone in the management echelons showed a certain concern about their image as a brutalizing, dehumanizing force in the world. Rodgers does not name the individual. He merely says that Tom Watson, the boss at IBM, was "unsuccessfully approached" in 1960 with an idea for creating a better public image. The idea involved the simulation of computerized designs for solving massive human problems such as housing, traffic congestion, city planning, etc. Apparently the suggestion was rejected on two grounds: human nature being what it is, people would probably consider such a simulation as an attempt to control or manipulate them; and it was thought that the corporation's success in materialistic terms was probably a more positive factor in the land of Ben Franklin and Horatio Alger than anything else could possibly be.[5]

It may be that the massive countercultural movement of young people in America in recent years is an indictment of both technology and materialism. It is undoubtedly directed against the technology of warfare as practiced in the Far East. But in its rejection of machine-produced furniture and clothing, prepackaged foods, and a Detroit-based economy, it appears to be responding negatively to a version of society that was becoming complicated and superorganized. Many young people have adopted a kind of Thoreauvian existence, attempting to reduce their necessities in order to resist being taken in by the technological society. One of their favorite epithets for anything they dislike, taken from the popular film *The Graduate,* has been the word "plastic." Something about their attempt to resist the cultural evolution is pathetic; but it is also admirable. In their willingness to cut across the grain, they keep alive something which we identify as basically human. It is hardly suprising that many of them have adopted Jesus as a kind of popular hero, not because of any religious tradition, but because he himself died for going against the grain.

### The Promise of Humanization

But not everyone fears technology as a dehumanizing force. On the contrary, there are some persons who say just the opposite, that it holds tremendous potential for making us more human. Machines are neutral, they say; they do not consciously conspire

5. Rodgers, op. cit., p. 325.

to take over the world. It is true that they provide a measure of power or leverage to unscrupulous persons as well as to scrupulous ones; but that is simply in the nature of things. What is important is that machines can drastically reduce the perils and problems of human existence and increase the pleasure in living.

What are the things that really dehumanize man, anyway? The answer is not machines, but poverty, hunger, illness, retardation, jealousy, theft, imprisonment—all products of want, mismanagement, and poor distribution which a fully computerized society could go far toward eliminating! Visit a real ghetto area sometime; smell the offensive odors emanating from behind apartment doors; observe the depressed expressions on the faces of men leaving for work or women shopping in the market; watch the children struggling to survive on the playground and in the streets. Or visit a jail; sit in a tiny cell with three men who are homosexuals and have no respect for themselves; eat in a chow line with two hundred other prisoners; stand around in the prison yard and feel the dejection of men whose every motion and look is watched by uniformed guards carrying guns. Or go to a hospital for the mentally ill; walk the wards and look at the aberrations from "acceptable" behavior; listen to the tales of injustice; try to get past the walls of silence and withdrawal; lie down on a table in an electroshock therapy room.

It could be complained, of course, that these are the derelicts of a technological society, the casualties of a war that was never declared. But it would not be true, for these phenomena are not new, nor are they coeval with industrialism. Society may tend to isolate its victims today, to cordon them off in specially designated areas more than it once did. But even that assumption is not entirely valid, as any student of history knows.

Socioeconomist Robert Theobald is representative of a number of persuasive voices saying today that the only real answer to the staggering social problems of man on this planet is a systems approach to management. We must be realistic, he says. Business corporations have been quick to see the importance of systems management in the coordination of their planning and growth; this accounts, in part, for the technological abuses we witness in society. What we must do now is to adopt the systems method in redressing the primary ills and pursuing the fundamental goals of mankind as a whole.

Man is a slave to the machine only if he wishes to be a slave. The machine, when it functions as intended, is actually an extension of man's being. It exists to extend his control over the environment, making it more habitable. If it has seemed to make it less so, that is the result of faulty planning and poor perspective. There is no reason why science should not make the world as amenable to human existence as it appears, say, in Huxley's *Brave New World,* only without destroying individual initiative and creativity in the way Huxley feared such a society might.

The problem, says Theobald, is that men have been lazy and have accepted the consequences of haphazard organization. We have permitted technological trends or accidents to make our decisions for us instead of using our intelligence to plan the trends. Now that certain men with visionary capacity see this, we have only to acquire political consensus to deal with our situation on a new holistic scale. We already have the technological capacity to ease the physical and economic burdens of most of the world's population.

"Man," writes Theobald, "will no longer need to toil; he must find a new role in the cybernetics era which must emerge from a new goal of self-fulfillment. He can no longer view himself as a superanimal at the center of the physical universe, nor as a superefficient taker of decisions self-fashioned in the model of the computer. He must now view himself as a truly creative being in the image of a creative God."[6]

6. Robert Theobald, "Cybernation and the Fulfillment of Man," *Liberation* (March 1965); reprinted in Hartsock, ed., op. cit., p. 329.

Buckminster Fuller concurs. In *Operating Manual for Spaceship Earth* he declares that the age of man's "specialization" is almost over. Heretofore, our being a race of specialists was required by the environmental situation. In Plato's *Republic* the ideal city-state was set up with a rigid stratification of special functions to be performed by citizens; in this way the city-state could operate economically and efficiently. But now, says Fuller, the machine has been developed to the point of taking over specializations. It performs them more readily and accurately than human beings. Nor should this be considered a put-down. On the contrary, specialization implies a kind of slavery. It limits the person practicing it. It involves a certain amount (frequently a great amount) of tedium. Now the computer can do the specialized work, freeing man to be a generalist, a combiner, a creator. The old idea of the "liberal" arts, so designated because only the free man could disregard more menial tasks and occupy himself with them, can at last be fulfilled in the general population.

The computer as superspecialist can persevere, day and night, day after day, in picking out the pink from the blue at superhumanly sustainable speeds. The computer can also operate in degrees of cold or heat at which man would perish. Man is going to be displaced altogether as a specialist by the computer. Man himself is being forced to reestablish, employ, and enjoy his innate "comprehensivity." Coping with the totality of Spaceship Earth and universe is ahead for all of us. Evolution is apparently intent that man fulfill a much greater destiny than that of being a simple muscle and reflex machine—a slave automaton—*automation* displaces the *automatons.*[7]

There, in a word, is the vision of the technetronic paradise! Man will be more fully man because he is no longer so completely subjugated to the physical environment. He will think, create, and enjoy like a god.

7. R. Buckminster Fuller, *Operating Manual for Spaceship Earth* (New York: Pocket Books, 1970), p. 40.

## The Science of Human Conditioning

There remains, however, the problem of the "fatal flaw" as the literature about tragic heroes used to call it. What is to guarantee man's use of the systems approach for his survival instead of his destruction? The bizarreness of *Dr. Strangelove* is hard to put out of our heads: suppose two rival systems developers emerge in the world and wage technetronic war on each other; we would all be blown back to the caveman stage of development in an instant, only with a scarred and gutted world to begin over in. In the end, contend many eminent scientists and psychologists, we must face realistically the problem of conditioning human behavior itself. Otherwise we shall live constantly with the ever-increasing danger of all our other technologies.

The best known, and in some ways most controversial, exponent of this attitude is Professor B. F. Skinner of Harvard University, designer of the teaching machine and programed learning, and the man whom *Time* magazine called "the most influential of living American psychologists."

Skinner has been preaching one message over and over again for years. It is a message taken up by hundreds of disciples around the world. And it is summed up in the opening paragraphs of his most recent book, *Beyond Freedom and Dignity:*

In trying to solve today's terrifying problems of war, over-population and pollution, we naturally play from strength, and our strength is science and technology. But while we have made many advances, things grow steadily worse, and it is disheartening to find that technology itself is increasingly at fault. War has acquired a new horror with the invention of nuclear weapons; sanitation and medicine have made the problems of population more acute, and the affluent pursuit of happiness is largely responsible for pollution.

Man must repair the damage or all is lost. And he can do so if he will recognize the nature of the difficulty. The application of the physical and biological sciences alone will not solve our problems because the solutions lie in another field.

What we need is a technology of behavior. We could solve our problems quickly enough if we could adjust the growth of the world's population as precisely as we adjust the course of a spaceship, or move toward a peaceful world with something like the steady progress with which physics has approached absolute zero (even though both presumably remain out of reach). But we do not have a behavioral technology comparable in power and precision to physical and biological technology, and those who do not find the very possibility ridiculous are more likely to be frightened by it than reassured.[8]

Twenty-five hundred years ago, says Skinner, man understood himself as well as he understood anything else in his world. Today he is what he understands least. Progress in the physical and biological sciences has been enormous since the days of Aristotle. But there has been no comparable development in the understanding of the self. We have continued to operate upon primitive premises about a mentalized being or soul as though the premises themselves were sacrosanct and could not be improved upon. Because of this, we have never dared to think that perhaps man is not really an autonomous being, a godlike creature who is a law unto himself.

All that we know from science, suggests Skinner, indicates that man is not so autonomous as he always supposed. As an infant at birth, he is already qualified in existence by hereditary factors. Within a few years he has been conditioned by external stimuli, including both punishments and rewards, to respond to environmental situations with certain habitual responses he can never completely abandon. His entire life, in fact, from cradle to grave, is a process of behavioral conditioning. Much of it is haphazard

8. B. F. Skinner, *Beyond Freedom and Dignity* (New York: Alfred A. Knopf, 1971), pp. 3–5. This citation is from the abridged version in *Psychology Today* (August 1971), p. 37.

and contradictory, to be sure; but it is conditioning nevertheless. Yet two primary myths remain uppermost in the human vocabulary: freedom and dignity.

These are not entirely reprehensible, Skinner admits. They have induced people through the ages to rebel against those who would control them by aversive methods. The literature of Sartre and Camus, for example, was effective propaganda against the tyranny of the Nazis in World War II.

But the myths have a negative effect when they become ends in themselves and stand between persons and their submission to benevolent control. They induce a state of permissiveness which allows unscrupulous persons or groups to mount their own selfish programs of control or aggrandizement.

In a sense, what Skinner is saying is that the "global village" of which McLuhan has spoken is here, and it is time to advance from a state of casual, unregulated kinds of conditioning to a calculated science of conditioning commensurate with the needs and maturity of the age in which we shall be living. He does not argue that we can produce overnight a system of worldwide human conditioning which has not evolved very far on its own in several millenia. But he does think we can recognize the need for such a system and begin to work at it in partial ways.

Part of such a program would be to recognize as a general fact the interrelatedness of everything that is in the world—human beings, institutional alignments, space, inorganic matter, extraterrestrial influences of various kinds, and everything else. It is a problem for man, says Skinner, that his skin demarcates him from the rest of the world in such a way as to give him the illusion that he is a self-sustained entity. The whole ecosystem would be better off today if we had realized all along how dependent we are on it and had promoted the proper flow of life *through* our selves instead of *in* ourselves.

## The Ultimate Election

The inescapable question about an otherwise reasonable proposal is: Who would be in charge of the conditioning, and who would be conditioned? The election of that individual, or group of individuals, would surely be the most important decision ever made by any part of the human species. It would invest the controller or controllers with a power hitherto only imagined in our society. He or they would make all decisions relative to the general welfare of society and would implement psychological conditioning for all human beings from birth to death.

Visions of Huxley's *Brave New World* or Orwell's *1984* rise like hideous specters to haunt such a possibility. Something in us instinctively rejects such a prospect as totalitarian and dehumanizing.

Skinner knows this and realizes the definite problems involved in establishing criteria for leadership in the conditioning/conditioned society. But he denies that the process would be dehumanizing. It would, only according to our former understandings of the meaning of humanity. Once we dispatch the myth of autonomous man, he says, we shall see that our true humanity is not jeopardized at all. (The argument of Theobald and Fuller for technological control of the physical world is thus extended to control of biology as well.)

Autonomous man, says Skinner, is a fiction, a device we use to explain what we once could explain in no other way.

We constructed him from our ignorance, and as our understanding increases, the very stuff of which he is composed vanishes. Science does not dehumanize man, it de-humunculizes him, and it must do so if it is to prevent the abolition of the human species.

To man *qua* man we readily say good riddance. Only by dispossessing autonomous man can we turn to the real causes of human behavior—

from the inferred to the observed, from the miraculous to the natural, from the inaccessible to the manipulable.[9]

Skinner had already dealt with most of the issues addressed by *Beyond Freedom and Dignity* in a fictional treatment in 1948. It was a utopian novel called *Walden Two,*[10] which presented an account of what a small community—in this case a thousand people—given to experimental control methods might look like. Camus once wrote that the philosophy of our time must be done in images, not in abstract language, which is why he wrote fictional counterparts of all his major philosophical books. He felt that images have more power to evoke action. Whether or not Skinner was following the same idea, *Walden Two* has proven to be extremely influential among recent generations of college students and has doubtless contributed to the founding of numerous communal societies intent on achieving the good life as Skinner outlined it.

Skinner admits that he dealt with both sides of his own personality in the novel by naming the designer of the Walden Two Community Frazier, for his own middle initial, and the professor of psychology who comes to visit the community Burris, for his own first name, Burrhus. Burris is skeptical about the community at first, primarily over the question of Frazier's qualifications for designing and executing it, but is finally won over and becomes a permanent member.

The question of electing a controller or controllers is solved in this instance by Frazier's having conceived the notion of a communal society and put it into action. New communities modeled on Walden Two are springing up in other parts of the country, and Frazier envisions a day when the majority of the world's people

9. Ibid., pp. 200–201; *Psychology Today,* p. 78.
10. B. F. Skinner, *Walden Two* (New York: Macmillan, 1970), quotations that follow are mainly from pp. 161 and 199.

will have been won over by the attractiveness of the life they offer and become a part of similar organizations.

Frazier emphasizes the fact that he is no longer necessary to Walden Two. As a member of the original board of directors of the community, he is scheduled to rotate off within a few months. None of the directors has much visibility to the community as a whole, and most members either do not recognize Frazier at all or do not associate him with the governing of the community. He cannot, therefore, be a despot in the utopia.

He does finally admit to Burris, however, that the control from his original design for the community persists and that in that sense he could be termed a despot. He even sees himself as a kind of Christ figure, or even as God. "Not a sparrow falleth," he remarks as he stands on a hill overlooking the community and surveys it with a spyglass. Burris accuses him of having quite a "sizable God-complex." Frazier readily admits it: it fulfills his power fantasies. He is not, after all, a true member of his own community. He has not been conditioned by it—at least, not entirely. He was the designer; it is an extension of his will.

Yet he pleads in his defense that everything has been done for the good of the members of the community. They live in ideal harmony. Work has been reduced to a minimum and is rewarded by a system of credits which puts a high premium on undesirable jobs. All tasks, buildings, equipment, and planning has been subjected to "cultural engineering" to insure a high quotient of efficiency. Maximum time and energy are left for the free enterprise of members, including reading, gardening, the arts, and human relationships. Children are reared communally, and give love to and receive it from all adult members of the community. Marriage is still honored as a relationship between the sexes, but the community helps young people to determine who they are best suited to wed. Undesirable traits are ignored lest they be reinforced and repeated, and desirable traits are reinforced in subtle yet effective manner.

When asked to define the good life, Frazier lists its ingredients: first, health, both emotional and physical; second, a minimum of unpleasant labor; third, a chance to exercise talents and abilities; fourth, intimate and satisfying personal contacts; and finally, relaxation and rest. Having these basic needs fulfilled, he says, reduces a person's tensions and permits him to enjoy life. The person no longer engages in a blind struggle to "have a good time" or "get what he wants." He exists in a true state of leisure.

There is no rational defense for such a life, says Frazier. "I can't give you a rational justification for any of it. I can't reduce it to any principle of 'the greatest good." This *is* the Good Life. We know it. It's a fact, not a theory. It has an experimental justification, not a rational one."

In the past, the good life has often been connected with some religious viewpoint or justification for it. But this is not true of Walden Two. As Frazier observes, "Our conception of man is not taken from theology but from a scientific examination of man himself."

## The Crucial Question

In Frazier's remark may lie the most crucial question to be asked of the whole technological control game, namely: Does man contain within himself sufficient goals for the fulfillment of his own nature, or do those goals lie quite beyond him? Supposing his inner goals to be sufficient, at what point in his evolution did they become so? Were they bound to become so? Or has theology itself shaped man in such a way as to make his "inner" goals inevitable to his fulfillment?

These are not easy queries to answer. Skinner assumes that we know what our goals are, that they are as visible almost as a bladder or a kidney might be if we were opened up. But how can we suppose, at this juncture in our evolution, that they are not somehow fundamentally theological in nature—that if there had been no theological engagement in the long history of man, we would not have sought quite different ends than the ones we now seek? And if we admit that our beginnings were all confused and intertwined with our religious yearnings and teachings, by what right do we foreswear them now? We cannot simply draw a line at this year or that and say, "Here, at this point, man no longer stands in fee to his religious past; he is now free to be himself and to posit his own goals." That is folly.

Frazier in *Walden Two* admits to Burris that he fancies himself a kind of Christ. Once he stretches out in a cruciform on the grass, consciously assuming the posture of the Messiah being put to death. He also confesses that there are "similarities" between him and God, though he supposes he has more control over his creation than God had over his. But this crucial psychological insight into Frazier (and perhaps into Skinner himself?) is formed on an analogy with our religious past; indeed, with the very heart of our religious past. The very metaphors that constitute his (Frazier's or Skinner's) power of imagery are derived immediately from the theological center. How can he even pretend to examine man scientifically without considering him inseparable from everything he has believed and loved? Who is fooling whom?

Granted for a moment that it were possible to isolate man and his goals from the religious context—from the fact that he has been called *homo religiosus*—there may be one more question of a practical nature. Our ideological natures have been more or less spoiled by the conception of God as a deity so characterized by selfless love as to have permitted his Son, his incarnation, to die for the sins of the world. The Lamb of God and all that. And we are, in most accounts, left as free moral agents to decide whether we will or will not accept such love.

The question then is: Can men who have been inspired by such a teaching ever settle for existence under the control of other human beings, whose selflessness could be no match for God's? It seems more likely that they would regard matters pretty much as Murphy did in Ken Kesey's *One Flew Over the Cuckoo's Nest.* Murphy recognized that the whole world was like the madhouse from which he was looking at things, and that it was full of Big Nurses whose control needs are simply insatiable. They will do anything, he observed—anything—to subjugate other people.

The picture Skinner paints is an attractive one. Indeed, it is so beatific as to suggest that the apocalyptic visions of Isaiah, of the lamb lying down with the lion and the bear with the ox might finally be pulled off by the right kind of conditioning.

It is hard to imagine a world [ he says] in which people live together without quarreling, maintain themselves by producing the food, shelter and clothing they need, enjoy themselves and contribute to the enjoyment of others in art, music, literature and games, consume only a reasonable part of the resources of the world and add as little as possible to its pollution, bear no more children than they can raise decently, continue to explore the world around them and discover better ways of dealing with it, and come to know themselves and the world around them accurately and comprehensively. Yet all this is possible. We have not yet seen what man can make of man.[11]

I personally find it difficult, if not impossible, to controvert Skinner's arguments. His reasoning is sane and cogent. But I think this well-armored giant has an Achilles' heel: he has made a myth of reasoning itself. Man, as William Barrett and others have been at pains to show us, is not a rational being. He may seem to be. He may conform to a line of reasoning for a considerable time and thus give the appearance of orderly progress. But then, whammo! He reaches a certain point and aberrates wildly! Were man a mere machine, with machinelike predictability, universal conditioning

11. Skinner, *Beyond Freedom,* p. 215; in *Psychology Today,* p. 80.

might one day usher in a Golden Age. But there is always a surd in the human situation, an irreducible factor, which produces unforeseen behavior.

Ionesco balances the picture somewhat with his portrait of man in *The Killer*. A demoniacal killer is stalking the City of Light, the apex of man's cultural engineering. Bérenger tracks him down and they face each other. Bérenger is surprised. The killer is not a fierce giant at all, but a small, apparently powerless creature. Bérenger decides to reason with him, to convince him that men ought to live and enjoy the City of Light, and thus to convert him from his asociality. As Bérenger musters argument after argument, the little killer only laughs a diabolical laugh. Gradually Bérenger weakens. His arguments begin to sound hollow even to himself. In the end, he submits to the killer, accepting his own death, because he can really think of no good reason to permit men to go on living and enjoying the City of Light.

Ionesco has described the sensations behind the composition of his play. He was walking through a French village about noon one day. It was in June, and the sun was casting an aura of pleasant warmth and laziness over everything. The noises of children playing and dogs barking floated to him over seas of dreaming. He was in a state of perfect euphoria. Suddenly, without warning, his mood changed. He felt threatened and paranoid. He experienced a kind of chill. This mercurial change, he decided, should provide the emotional graph for a play.

This picture is truer to man as I know him than Skinner's is. Admittedly, Skinner could give some powerful arguments against the illustration. Ionesco, he would probably contend, is the product of poor conditioning. And it would be easy enough to verify such a contention from biographical fragments in Ionesco's journals. But it is one thing to imagine that Ionesco would have been more stable had he received proper conditioning, and quite another thing to suppose that even the most sophisticated human engineering would have turned him into an exemplary member of Walden Two.

The story of the Garden of Eden and the myth of man's imperfectibility even there cannot be sneezed out of the picture. It probably contains a kind of wisdom an optimistic technological viewpoint should bear in mind. Salvation by progress, now hopefully accelerated by the advent of cybernetics, is important too. There is no reason why it should not improve the quality of human existence and bring us closer to the Old Testament ideal of a unified people dwelling harmoniously in a land flowing with milk and honey. But we should not lose our perspective. There are dimensions—mysteries—in the human story for which it may never offer a satisfactory account. Even if we should succeed in stripping away the functions once assigned to autonomous man, as Skinner suggests we ought, and transferring them one by one to the controlling environment, one fact remains, irreducible to mere logic: the whole is often more than its parts.

It would be hard to conceive of an engineered society more technically perfect than the one Huxley described forty years ago in *Brave New World*. It is also hard to forget the Savage's protest against such a world of sterility and technological convenience: "But I don't want comfort. I want God. I want poetry, I want real danger, I want freedom, I want goodness. I want sin."

# 5

# Groupies and the Kingdom

At the time of this writing Thomas Harris's *I'm OK—You're OK* is on the national bestseller list and has been there for many weeks.[1] Harris is a disciple of Eric Berne, the famous Games-People-Play psychiatrist, and is part of the Transactional Analysis school of psychotherapy. TA, as it is called, is more concerned about the everyday functioning of human beings than it is about ferreting out minute details of their infantile neuroses. By analyzing how people respond to other persons in the routine encounters or transactions of life, it promises to help them actually change their ways of responding. Evidently many people feel the need to change.

The core of TA is a distinction among three types of reaction common to every one of us. These are the reactions of the Child, the Parent, and the Adult. Childish reactions are primarily at the feeling level. They are instinctual, unpremeditated, and unlearned. Parental reactions, on the other hand, are those we have learned by observing and imitating parents or society in general. They

1. Thomas Harris, *I'm OK—You're OK* (New York: Harper & Row, 1969).

have to do with the rules and regulations of life, with keeping order, and with preserving moral or ethical codes. Adult reactions are those arrived at after weighing inclinations to both childish and parental reactions and deciding what would really be best in the situation.

The goal is to measure each transaction and then produce adult behavior. Harris assures us that we're well on the way to the goal once we have got into the habit of recognizing which part of ourselves—Child, Parent, Adult—is responsible for the response we are about to make to a given stimulus. It is reacting without thinking that involves us in most of our difficulties. It is possible, of course, for a person to be a "Child-contaminated Adult" or a "Parent-contaminated Adult," so that his Adult picture of a situation is never clear. In that case, he is psychotic and needs individual attention from a therapist. But most people struggle with simple neurotic problems which can be eased with a little experience at TA.

A parent can learn, for example, not to respond to the Child in his or her child with the Child in himself. Temper tantrums are not best met by more temper tantrums. The wise parent knows also not to respond to a child with the unreflective Parent side of his nature. That is merely pulling rank and citing the rule book, which may or may not be appropriate in the instance. Instead, the parent analyzes the situation, sees that the child needs stroking (a favorite term of Harris's to mean "reassuring" or "giving security"), decides whether the Parent reaction would be helpful at this time, and then responds to the child accordingly.

Even teenagers and preteenagers should be acquainted with the language and methods of TA, says Harris. Learning to cope with their emotional problems in an intelligent manner ought to be made part of their educational curriculum. It is shortsighted of us to concentrate so totally on equipping them to make a living and give them so little training in how to relate to other persons and enjoy life.

## Learning to Feel OK

Most of us know far too little about relating to other persons. What we do know we have picked up from experience, and most of it is wrong because we picked it up before we had enough data and perspective to analyze it fairly.

This is why psychoanalysis is so concerned with a person's childhood. It is during the earliest years of life, as Freud demonstrated, that we decide what other people are like and what we must do to survive among them. We learn most from our parents or parent surrogates. If they are wise and loving enough, we believe the world is to be trusted and we respond to it happily. If they are not, we become suspicious. We may even learn to be deceitful. After all, we are organisms, we have not yet learned ethical or moral values, and we are bent on surviving.

There are organic problems, such as chemical or hormonal imbalance, which can also account for distressed behavior, and this is why analysts must receive training as medical doctors as well as therapists. But most emotional dysfunction in our lives is traceable to faulty response patterns which were established before we could even read or write.

For many years psychoanalysts seemed preoccupied with verifying their theories about the origins of neuroses. Consequently they worked primarily with persons whose manifestations of problems were most severe. Now there is considerable interest in the other direction, in applying what has been learned about human personality to the millions of more or less average persons who have not had breakdowns or functional disabilities but who could be helped to enjoy life more completely.

"To oversimplify the matter somewhat," says Abraham Maslow, "it is as if Freud supplied to us the sick half of psychology and we must now fill it out with the healthy half."[2]

The major object of Maslow's own work has been to discover and analyze what he calls the "self-actualizing" person, the person who lives in a self-fulfilling way all the time and not merely in occasional moments of "peak experience." All people are self-actualizing at times of peak experience, he says; when something occurs which excites them, they suddenly come in contact with their true identities. The full-time self-actualizer, though, is excited by everything. Life is continually joyous to him, and he lives in more or less constant touch with his selfhood.

Not only that, but he functions more independently than other persons. He requires less external supplying of such basic needs as love, food, shelter, respect, and praise. He is more able to give love and respect for themselves alone and not as payment for what he wants in return. He radiates playfulness and creativity. The word "radiate," in fact, is characteristic of him; life seems to emanate from him, to come out along the radii that center in his person.

Getting people who are not self-actualizers to become so is of course far from easy. Psychology does not hope for the kind of radical conversion evangelistic religion has talked so much about. At best, a modification of response patterns is aimed for. Once the individual has received some perspective on his way of behavior, he is encouraged to deal more warily with the stimuli that produce undesirable reactions in him. But because most responses are automatic and immediate, there is often little time for him to put his acquired knowledge into play. Therefore retraining himself in altered patterns is discouragingly slow.

The appealing factor about Harris's book is the simplified schema he has devised for acquainting the average reader with his

2. Abraham Maslow, *Toward a Psychology of Being* (New York: Van Nostrand-Reinhold Co., 1968), p. 5.

own attitudinal and behavioral possibilities. There are only four basic patterns of attitude toward the self and its external world, according to Harris:

> I'M NOT OK—YOU'RE OK
> I'M NOT OK—YOU'RE NOT OK
> I'M OK—YOU'RE NOT OK
> I'M OK—YOU'RE OK

Harris is unequivocal in his assertion that the I'M NOT OK attitude is universal in small children. During the earliest years there are usually strong OK feelings too, induced by the physical stroking the child receives. But as he receives less and less stroking and enters increasingly into an adult world, he measures himself against the size, power, and authority of grownups or larger children and decides he is basically NOT OK

The I'M NOT OK—YOU'RE NOT OK position occurs in children who suddenly lose the stroking they were receiving. This commonly happens at the end of the first year of life when the child begins to walk and is carried about less than in early infancy. In addition to being fondled less than before, he also experiences stricter punishment because he is moving about and getting into more things. His own NOT OK feelings are reinforced, and he feels disappointed in the parent, who is also NOT OK. If this position is not altered, the person may eventually end up in a state of extreme withdrawal, regressing emotionally to earliest infancy in search of the only stroking he ever knew.

If the child is brutalized or severely hurt by the adults in his life, he may suddenly switch from his NOT OK to an OK position in which he says I'M OK—YOU'RE NOT OK. This is a life-saving move for him, says Harris; it means survival. If unchecked, it can also develop into an attitude of toughness and cruelty, and the person may become a criminal psychopath, treating other persons, who are NOT OK, in any way he wishes.

The real hope both for society and the individual is the fourth position, I'M OK—YOU'RE OK. It is a position qualitatively different from the other three. Those positions are all unconscious, but this one is the product of the Adult, reasoning mind. Most people go through life in the first position. Some unfortunate children move to the second or third position. By the end of the third year of life, says Harris, one of these three positions is fixed in every person. The fourth, or I'M OK—YOU'RE OK, position is based on additional gathering of information about the self and the world, as well as on the help of religion and philosophy. The first three positions are based on feeling; the fourth is the result of thought, faith, and decision.

Now what can help the individual who says I'M NOT OK— YOU'RE OK to decide to change his position to I'M OK—YOU'RE OK? Remember, this is the position of the average person. Persons in the other two positions, I'M NOT OK—YOU'RE NOT OK and I'M OK —YOU'RE NOT OK, usually require psychiatric attention. But Harris's book is written especially for the I'M NOT OK—YOU'RE OK person, who feels that he is inadequate and ineffectual in a world where many people are better or more attractive. For the millions of such persons who are not living at full potential because they put themselves down, he recommends a functional knowledge and practice of Transactional Analysis; and he further recommends that it be learned and practiced in a group.

## The Importance of Groups

Harris is strong on groups for two reasons. The first is that groups are an economical approach to psychological help. Good psychiatrists can see only a fraction of the people who seek their help; they simply haven't time for everybody. And many people cannot afford individual psychoanalysis.

The second reason is that NOT OK people need the presence of several other persons in therapy with them. In TA, other persons help to identify the PAC, or Parent-Adult-Child, roles the patient is playing. They are often as adept at picking up on these as the trained therapist. Also, hearing other persons verbalizing their own position difficulties enables the individual to realize that his feeling of worthlessness or inadequacy is quite common. He is more readily motivated to decide that he is OK after all and to practice an I'M OK attitude.

It is surprising too how generous people tend to become in their support of people in therapy groups who deserve it. Often the person who has gone through life with a stroking-deprivation discovers that these people who were entirely unknown to him before the beginning of the sessions are able to stroke him. He is filled with strange and wonderful feelings which he may not have felt since the first year of infancy. Even if he has had his share of stroking from family members or old friends, but could not accept it as genuine, it means something to him that people who were complete strangers before the sessions find him acceptable.

This positive or curative effect of the group was first explored with any significance several decades ago by J. L. Moreno, a Viennese psychiatrist who was especially interested in psychodrama and founded the Psychodramatic Institute of New York. Moreno found it helpful to many of his patients to play roles together. Sometimes they played their own roles, recalling a childhood anxiety and acting it out against a surrogate parent. Other times they exchanged roles and acted out strange parts, usually with enlightening results.

In 1946 three men who had been influenced by Moreno's work, Leland Bradford, Ronald Lippitt, and Kenneth Benne, established the National Training Laboratories in Bethel, Maine. The NTL at that time was primarily interested in studying the dynamics of groups in process and training instituitonal and corporation personnel in methods of group management. In the early fifties, T-groups (for training groups) became more concerned for individual awareness, and the term "sensitivity training" became popular among them. Then, as personal therapy through group meetings became increasingly extensive through the influence of such therapists as Carl Rogers and Frederick Perls, the term "encounter group" gained wide recognition. William Schutz, who worked with Perls at Esalen, prefers the term "open encounter group" because it expresses the free, unfettered nature of such meetings and the willingness of the leaders to try anything at the moment that might improve the quality of the therapy.

There are numerous variations of the encounter group. Some are led by legitimate psychiatrists or trained counselors, some by self-professed gurus, some by schoolteachers, some by ministers, some by social workers. Occasionally one hears of a group that is functioning without a leader. They are sponsored by schools, churches, business corporations, and private foundations. It is estimated that some two million persons in the United States alone have now had at least one intensive group experience. When one is familiar with the techniques of encounter practiced in groups it is possible to see the widespread effects of this experience, especially in the communication media. There is a sense in which we are on the way to becoming an encounter culture.

Most groups are small. Ten or twelve persons are considered optimal by most leaders. They may meet for brief "microlabs," for extended sessions over several months' time, or for marathon sessions in which participants go for 24 to 72 hours with only such sleep as can be had right in the room where the group is meeting.

The emphasis in each meeting is on the interaction of the participants. The leader or therapist is not present to make speeches or take notes or correct mistaken ideas. He is there in the role of a facilitator to make suggestions, encourage participation, or even react personally like the other participants. It is possible for a group to spend an entire evening together without the leader's speaking once. It is also possible that the group will turn on the leader and discuss his personality hang-ups. Some therapists are know to react negatively toward the whole idea of group sessions for this reason.

Each person is urged to communicate his *feelings* to the group, not his opinions or rational thoughts. "Bull!" someone is liable to shout during a person's analysis of some situation. "Don't tell us what you think. We can all think. Tell us what you feel!"

Similarly, there is strong emphasis on the *now* as opposed to what was or what might be. A person may be stopped in the middle of reciting a childhood memory and asked to concentrate on what he is feeling right at the moment. The shock of the present tense is often great to a person who has preferred living in the past or dreaming of the future to facing the realities of the moment. It may be difficult for him to look into the demanding faces of fellow groupies and verbalize how he feels about them, about the room, about the situation he is in. But it is considered a major step forward when he learns to do it.

Obviously there is a high premium on honesty in the group session. Fantasizing, lying, or "faking it" simply are not permitted. Groups exhibit an uncanny facility for spotting falsity and attacking it until it is eradicated. I remember a group meeting in which a young woman unflinchingly went after an intelligent lawyer in the group. She said she had never known who he was because he always wore a mask. He replied with some indignation that his profession required the wearing of a mask, and that, to tell the truth, he himself probably didn't know who he was without a mask. The battle between them raged for an hour, with other persons taking the woman's part against the lawyer, and ended only when she was exhausted and said, "Okay, I wanted to help you, but you kept the door locked."

Schutz, in *Here Comes Everybody,* speaks of the high physical-ity quotient groups assume. Our society is characterized by sensory or sensual deprivation, despite all the pornography stands and X-rated movies, which are only lurid symptoms of the deprivation. Consequently people are uptight about physical expression of interpersonal feelings and seldom use their bodies to say what bodies can say very eloquently. Schutz therefore favors nudity in group meetings—because, as he says, there is little point in keeping other secrets once the body's secrets have been disclosed. He has even gone so far in his groups as to have the men compare the sizes of their penises and to conduct group examinations of women's vaginal cavities. This seems excessive, but again I understand his point. If honesty in sexual matters can be arrived at, with all the social taboo there is against it, then honesty in other matters ought to be purchased more easily.

Physicality in the average group takes much more modest forms. I have noticed about posture, for example, that as encounters become more intimate and people become more involved, one or two persons will leave their chairs and move to the floor. Before long, others follow the lead. Often a whole group that began by sitting on sofas and chairs will have moved to the carpet or floor before the evening is over. Intimacy is also signaled by the manner of dress. The more intense the encounter, the more casual the mode of dress becomes. Even in a meeting of corporation executives which may have begun with participants in ties and shirtsleeves, there will be a loosening of ties, rolling up of sleeves, and jettisoning of shoes. Most important of all, there is invariably a relaxation of the taboo about touching other persons. Occasionally aggression is manifested in pushing or slapping. More frequently, however, friendship and support become communicated through patting, hugging, or kissing. Interestingly, in a culture which has placed even more taboo on embracing between men than on their embracing of women, there is normally in a meeting a breaking down of reserve that results in males being free to hug males.

As Harris says in *I'm Ok—You're Ok* the important thing that happens in groups, once the honesty level is reached, is the stroking that approval-starved individuals get. In a true encounter session, a person knows that the strokes are not false. They are not like the idle compliments paid among socialites or civic leaders. They are the expression of real feelings. And they are not unmixed with criticism and gutsy appraisal. They have meaning and value because they are produced in a setting which is sudden death on falsehood and hypocrisy.

The individual comes out of such sessions with, perhaps for the first time in his entire life, an intelligent picture of how he is viewed and reacted to by other people. The experience has been for him like a 360-degree talking mirror—he has seen himself as others see him. The value of this in a society characterized by mobility, institutionalism, and anonymity may be simply incalculable, for where else can a person count on an honest appraisal in such a society? Almost all our involvements outside the family, says Hendrik Ruitenbeek, author of *The New Group Therapies,* are with secondary and tertiary groups—PTA's, car pools, Sunday-school classes, office forces, civic clubs, etc. There are almost no primary groups—groups born of long-term, intimate involvement and personal care—remaining in contemporary society. Yet nowhere except in the primary group does the individual receive the kind of total feedback necessary for him to know who he really is. What the encounter group offers, then, is a kind of instant intimacy. It restores the individual's picture of himself, enabling him to function in a general society that not only ignores him but seems at times to be out to get him.

### The Excitement Generated by the Group Approach

There are detractors and debunkers of the encounter movement, as there are of any movement engaging in radical or controversial practices. But there are more enthusiasts than detractors, if one may judge from the number of books and articles that continue to flow from the pens of both therapists and journalists who have taken part in group experiences.

One of the richest fields for the encounter method appears to have been turned up in the local church. All over the country ministers and church-going psychologists have been praising it as the most promising method of spiritual renewal to come down he road in ages, if not in centuries. The church, they say, was dying of institutional senescence. The gray fog of impersonality that has settled on government, corporate existence, and just about everything else in this country, has made no exception of the church, especially in the larger churches afflicted by far-flung parish memberships, large, specialty-trained staffs, and the general problems of social anonymity. The ready intimacy of the small group, it is claimed, offsets this paralyzing, immobilizing situation. Sometime in combination with biblical studies, topical investigations, or prayer times, and sometimes in their purest and rawest forms as encounter sessions, these groups are beginning to spread and to honeycomb the innter structures of numerous churches.

Typical of the encomia heaped on the group approach is this paragraph from a book by Howard Clinebell, who is Professor of Pastoral Care at Claremont Theological Seminary in California:

> In the small, sharing group lies the power which enables persons to love more fully and live more creatively. This is the *people dynamic— the power we have to recreate each other and ourselves through caring and sharing.* Growth groups offer a means of releasing the people dynamic to help humanize personal relationships and to help create a world in which every person will have the opportunity to develop his full, unique capacities.[3]

Gerald Jud, who is head of the Department of Evangelism for the United Church of Christ, devotes most of his time now to

3. Howard Clinebell, *The People Dynamic* (New York; Harper & Row, 1972), p. viii.

conducting weekend encounter sessions. We have tried everything we know to revive the failing structures of the ecclesiastical institution, he says, and it has all failed. "A renewed church will emerge when in some deep sense we are a new people; when something equivalent to the early eighteenth-century's Great Awakening stirs us to our roots; when Pentecost is again the common experience of the church."[4] The Human Potential Movement, for Jud, offers a contemporary form for that Pentecost. He and his wife, who is a psychologist, are deeply immersed in it. "On a frontier, we do not wish to make undue claims," he says, "but we do want to bear our excited witness to what we have seen and heard and felt. We hope the Church will listen. If the church does not pay attention to this important movement, once again the Master will have come in disguise and the church will have failed to recognize him."[5]

This kind of enthusiasm, and particularly the reference to the Great Awakening, is especially interesting in the light of a recent critique of the encounter movement by Thomas C. Oden called *The Intensive Group Experience: The New Pietism.* Noting that the strong emphasis on the here and now in encounter circles tends to produce a kind of antihistoricism in groupies, Oden counters the tendency by examining the contemporary phenomenon in the light of movements which have borne a resemblance to it in earlier centuries. His conclusion is that there are striking similarities between the language and practices of today's groups and those of pietistic sects within both Christianity and Judaism. The most obvious parallels are with classic Protestant pietism and Jewish Hasidism in the seventeenth and eighteenth centuries, particularly with the developments from Spener, Zinzendorf, and the Baal Shem-Tob.

4. Gerald J. and Elisabeth Jud, *Training in the Art of Loving: The Church and the Human Potential Movement* (Philadelphia: Pilgrim Press, 1972), p. 11.
5. Ibid., p. 14.

Oden is sympathetic with the encounter culture and does not attempt to put it down by comparing it with movements in the past. He reminds us that classic pietism was a much more creative and virile experiential movement than the deteriorated forms it sank into in nineteenth- and twentieth-century religious settings such as evangelicalism, fundamentalism, and Jewish orthodoxy. The very word "piety" has been so contaminated by association with false or showy devotion that today it has primarily negative connotations.

But the points of comparison between the new group experience and the Spener-Zinzendorf variety of pietism are numerous. As Oden says, early Protestant and Jewish pietism emphasized

"here and now" experiencing, intensive small-group encounter, high trust levels in group interaction, honest confession amid a caring community, experimental mysticism, mutual pastoral care, extended conversion marathons, radical accountabiltiy to the group, an eclectic amalgam of resources for spiritual formation, intimate personal testimony, gut-level self-disclosure, brutally candid feedback procedures, anti-establishment social attitudes, and the laicization of leadership.[6]

It is difficult not to believe, in the face of the evidence, that the church has long been prepared, albeit unwittingly, for the current outbreak of encounter methods in its midst, and that the group culture outside the churches is actually only a secularized and demythologized form of something long ago foreshadowed in religious circles.

Oden actually lines up in parallel columns citations from the writings and sayings of leading pietists, including John Wesley, and the major contemporary therapists. The effect is overwhelming, for the language and emphases are often almost identical.

This basic structural and emotional relationship between the

6. Thomas C. Oden, *The Intensive Group Experience: The New Pietism* (Philadelphia: Westminster Press, 1972), pp. 56-57.

two movements, religious and secular, may account in part for the mystical fervor which even nonreligious persons appear to attach to the encounter experience. The multiple sense of self-awareness, self-identity, and self-transcendence which many people arrive at in the group process is, at the emtotional level at least, akin to what is felt in religious circles as a spiritual experience.

Schutz, who confesses that he began encounter work as a nontheistic Jew, speaks glowingly in *Here Comes Everybody* of the feeling of "presence" he has discovered in groups:

> When the encounter gets more advanced, say, to include meditation, then mystical experiences begin occurring even more frequently. Combining the encounter group with the religious experience has helped me to elevate my aspirations for the encounter group. To look for the God in man and to get in touch with his cosmic energy are becoming meaningful phrases to me and seem to transcend what I had earlier taken as encounter goals. Similarly, looking at interpersonal states in terms of energy exchanges is a religious experience that I can often feel.[7]

It is interesting to note, too, the pattern of evangelistic concern for the world that runs through the encounter movements in both church and secular society.

Clinebell envisions the encounter group as a model for social change in families, schools, and social agencies. The last chapter of *The People Dynamic* is entitled "Training Change Agents to Humanize Society."

And Schutz, whose concern in the earlier book *Joy: Expanding Human Awareness* seemed to lie primarily with the individual, has widened his interest in *Here Comes Everybody* to the entire social context. In the latter book he includes imaginary encounter dialogues for married couples, office workers and administrators, political stiuations, and educational settings. He even has a fantas-

7. William Schutz, *Here Comes Everybody* (New York: Harper & Row, 1971), p. 281.

tic encounter script for a summit conference between the leaders of the United States and the USSR in which the therapist and the Russian premier arm-wrestle on the floor and all the participants are shaken to the core by the experience of reacting to each other as persons and not as political representatives!

## The Big Question

I personally believe that the encounter culture is a revitalizing agency in our society and that its significance is enormous. We have all experienced the tendency of society, under the pressures of industrialization and technicalization, to become entropic, or increasingly dispersed. A sense of aloneness, of alienation, has characterized the works of many of our greatest artists—Melville, Hardy, James, Baudelaire, Hemingway, Kafka, Rilke, Camus, Robbe-Grillet, and many others. If people have responded enthusiastically to the sense of intimacy and relationship they have discovered in groups, it is because these were so desperately absent from their existence before.

But is the group experience the big answer we've been looking for? We have noted its similarity to the religious experience of earlier times. Is it, then, the way of salvation for man today?

I am inclined to say both Yes and No.

On the Yes side, it is extremely important for us to rediscover who we are in the human context and to learn how to relate to others at the level of honesty and care. The biblical notion of love, consummately symbolized in the Johannine interpretation of Christ's death, has doubtless transformed the world. But even that noble doctrine becomes hollow when persons are so emotionally paralyzed or crippled by the conditions of society that they must deal with other human beings in false or fabricated ways. The encounter movement, whether in the church or out of it, has helped to make relationships functional again for many people.

And the promise it extends for achieving a new level of integrity and openness in society as a whole is considerable.

Having participated in a group myself, I have great respect for the encounter process and the way it "shakes down" relationships, isolating and eliminating falsehood and role-playing. In the right setting, people have an uncanny facility for going to the heart of any matter and treating it almost clinically, so that, if embarrassment or fear is present it is soon dispelled.

The eminent psychologist Carl Rogers has commented in a similar vein:

> I trust the group, given a reasonably facilitating climate, to devleop its own potential and that of its members. For me, this capacity of the group is an awesome thing. Perhaps as a corollary of this, I have gradually developed a great deal of trust in the group process. This is undoubtedly similar to the trust I came to have in the process of therapy in the individual, when it was facilitated rather than directed. To me the group seems like an organism, having a sense of its own direction even though it could not define that direction intellectually.[8]

As a sort of stage-door theologian too, I am delighted to see group therapy's secularization of the doctrine of grace make that enormously significant doctrine available to persons in terms which they can grasp and utilize. Harris, in I'M OK—YOU'RE OK regards the movement from the I'M NOT OK feeling to the I'M OK position as constituting essentially the same experience in the individual as discovering that he is acceptable to the moral God of the universe. He cites the idea of Paul Tillich that Christian grace is accepting the fact that one is accepted, and says that this is the goal of most therapy, to persuade people to entrust themselves, with all their faults and blemishes, to the world around them. Obviously many Christians who speak of grace quite easily

8. Carl Rogers, *Carl Rogers on Ecounter Groups* (New York: Harper & Row, 1970), p. 44.

—and this includes ministers—have only a conceptual and not a functional experience with it. The group reifies and makes actual the forgiveness which religion, in many cases, has managed only to institutionalize.

On the other hand—the No side—I have a reservation, especially about groups which operate in the secular context. It is rather intangible, and I shall probably express it poorly, but I must try.

For all the respect in which I hold group therapy and its demythologizing of religious doctrine, I harbor a certain fear that it is unable to cure the ideological diffuseness which is part of the modern distemper. Thus, I want to be as mature in my religious views as possible; no more fountain squares. No more fundamentalist plans of salvation. Yet even in my maturity I realize that something has gone—call it a sense of magic or mystery—when the old myths that served the religious urgency in man no longer do so. In Harris's terminology, I pass from the state of the Child, which may be the condition for religion, to the state of the Adult, which is the province of theology and philosophy. I no longer act or worship impulsively and unreflectively—or at least I do so more seldom. No I see myself acting as I do; I have perspective; and the perspective gives me pause. Why do I believe as I do? What am I doing when I pray? Is God the greatest reality, the *ens realissimum,* or is he a projection of all human finitude and its fantasy, including my own? You see, there is no more *actus purus* for me. All my thinking and acting is contaminated by the cautiousness of my Adult.

And I suspect that this is precisely where much of the modern problem, on its philosophical or religious side, got its start. There was very little of the Who-am-I-why-am-I-here? syndrome around up until the last two centuries. Its development has been coeval with the rise of the historical criticism of the scriptures and the calling in question of the ancient structures of theology and the

Church. As long as the existence of God was unquestioned, the nature and duty of man were unquestioned. Man was created, as Calvin said, *in imago Dei*—in the image of God—and his only duty was to do the will of God.

Once there began to be wholesale defection from the assumptions of theism, however, there was no longer any guarantee of the nature of humanity. When the seawall guarding the definition broke, there was no stopping the erosion. The modern experience has consequently been one of wandering and anxiety. The poet Hölderlin characterized it as a kind of cosmic "homelessness" in which man has been permanently orphaned. Martin Heidegger, the German philosopher, has spoken of our *Gewörfenheit* or "thrownness," as though we were tossed onto a giant stage without author, script, or audience. The human condition is one vast identity crisis. As Herman Hesse wrote in the prologue to his novel *Demian,* "What a real living human being is made of seems to be less understood today than at any time before."

This is the reason for the almost subhuman character of the personae in Beckett's *Godot* and other plays. If they knew who Godot was—or God—they would have some handle on their own situation. But they don't and they haven't.

Secularity, masking as freedom, may have become a kind of myth in its own right. If so, it may impart a temporary content to the meaning of humanity and the state of being human. But inasmuch as it is itself only a state of existence antithetical to that of religion and the religious world view, it can hardly be considered ultimate. Someday it too must give way before the demythologizers.

Alain Robbe-Grillet, the French screenwriter, novelist, and critic, for example, already complains that the existential humanism of Sartre and Camus failed to follow through on its dereligionizing of man. It refused God, he says, but did not accept the full consequences of such a refusal. It tried to keep the world as man had known it under theism. But it isn't only existentialism that is at fault. Any form of humanism, says Robbe-Grillet, is an attempt to "recover *everything*"—that is, to preserve the relationship between man and his world that we had under the old traditions. We must take more seriously the postulate that there is no relationship and that there is no such thing as "human nature." Man is a form of conscious life in the universe, and that is all we should say about him. The idea that there is any intrinsic relationship between him and the world his eyes look out upon is mere superstition, and must be left behind.[9]

The point I am awkwardly trying to make is that encounter groups in and by themselves, can hardly cope with the ideological problems that lie behind some of the basic behavioral difficulties the groups do try to address. The loss of cultural centrality that resulted from the demise of Christendom is a major cause of the nameless personal anxieties that afflict us today. The encounter culture helps us to deal with these anxieties in a functional, piecemeal way, but without the help of Church or some other mythologizing agency is powerless to get at the root of the matter: namely, the great loss.

A small illustration of this failure to handle the root problem may be seen in the dependency that groupies often feel toward their groups. Because their ideological deficiencies have not been affected by encounter methods, many persons are unable to transfer the authority for living from the group to the external world. Consequently they run about the country searching for new groups to relate to. Like superficially religious persons who require frequent revivals to keep their spiritual zeal stoked, they are at their happiest only in the context of the group.

In church groups, the failure seems usually to be offset by the

9. Alain Robbe-Grillet, *For a New Novel,* trans. Richard Howard (New York: Grove Press, 1965), pp. 49-75.

tacit assumption that there is a body of mytholgical imagery or truth standing behind the participants. Rarely verbalized, this assumption surfaces occasionally as the validation of human relationships in moments of unusual stress or resolution. At such times it often has the force of a mystical insight, transcending and crowning the participants' struggles.

I remember, for example, a night of especially stringent encounter in a church group, when several persons spoke honestly for the first time ever about their true feelings for each other. Many defenses were shattered, and the level of explicitness was very rare. There was a general feeling of shock and compulsion, and several persons, including some of the men, wept. Before the session was over, however, there was much embracing and kissing, and many said that they had never felt the presence of Christ more powerfully. It was as though the metaphysic of the church had stood at the center of all that happened as its genuinely cohesive power, and the recovery of this metaphysic, as much as the recovery of human relationship, was celebrated in individual lives in the days following.

Perhaps it is the unconscious desire for something like this metaphysic to guarantee the validity of relationships that has led secular therapists like Schutz to speak of the encounter experience in terms of transcendence and the exchange of cosmic energy.

I hope I am not misunderstood as denying the importance of even the secular encounter group. As I said, I am convinced of the significance of its therapeutic contribution to human existence, whatever its source. Therapy is therapy, with or without sectarian labels.

It is only that the salvation of human beings, since those beings are not simple creatures, is not a simple matter and must be prosecuted on many fronts at once. The encounter movement is operative on one or more of those fronts and is doing a splendid job. Its effect is so striking for many persons as to require the use of superlatives. They may even describe it as being redemptive in their cases. But the salvation of Man—of the genus—of the human context—requires that we see it in some perspective and pursue other modes as well.

# 6

# Religion and the Body Electric

It is important what the sun said on Sam Keen's shoulders. Keen had been a professor at Louisville Presbyterian Theological Seminary. Philosophy of religion. Modestly successful in his vocation, with two published books under his belt. But apparently something was lacking. Keen took a sabbatical. Instead of going to Germany, like most theologians, he went to Big Sur country, to Esalen Institute. Sensitivity training, group meetings, physical therapy, time to relax. Time to *feel*.

While he was at Esalen, Keen worked on *To a Dancing God.* What the sun said is in the last chapter of that book.

It had been a bad night. Keen had tossed and turned— "in exile," as he puts it, with demons from his ancient past returning to destroy hope. Rising, he sat facing the sea, with the pounding of the surf in his temples. Slowly the gentle heat of the early sun spread across his back, massaging it. His breathing became measured and slow. His body relaxed. The demons left. The day began—"gracefully."

How should he understand what had happened? he pondered. Nothing in his theology spoke to the way the sun had exercised the demons. Theology simply did not deal with the *carnality* of

**114**

grace. Rummaging on the other side of his background, he realized that secular ideologies were of no help either; they had not provided him with any categories for understanding the *grace* of carnality. It was a standoff. For one reason or another, man had simply failed to break through to a real comprehension of the meaning of salvation through incarnation. Christianity had by-and-large succumbed to the heresy of Gnosticism, which considers the mind or spirit of man to be inherently more important than the body.

Keen did not return to his seminary. He is now Professor of the Person at Prescott College in Arizona and a roving editor for *Psychology Today* magazine. He is reputed to be working on a book about the theology of carnality. I imagine the sun is still speaking to him, and sometimes I envy his break with the more formal world of theology.

## The Revolution We Are In

The conversion of Sam Keen and the flurry of interest in his somatic theology are, of course, rather minor items in any larger report on contemporary sensuality. They have significance to the theological community because the flesh is feared most in that circle. They have a symbolical importance, like tattered flags still flying at dawn or a spidery crack in a long seawall. But the world at large is far ahead of the Church and theologians in the return to the body.

We are, in fact, in the midst of a radical transition, with profound and far-reaching effects for the future of man and his way of regarding himself. The long centuries of Christendom's sway, in which the body was regarded with suspicion and even hostility, are essentially over. Now it is the mind, the intellect, the organizing faculty, that is becoming suspect. Freud, more than anyone, made us aware of the way we are manipulated and controlled by our superegos. Therefore we are inclined to distrust the superego.

Our egalitarian sympathies are aroused for the body, whose requirements are direct and less complicated.

Whitman's celebration of the body has proved more prophetic than anyone a century ago could have realized. We are entering the age of the body, of the total person, of the Gestalt being. The mind or intellect, which Platonism and Platonic Christianity taught us to be the highest form of the self—the godlike part of man—is seen in its dependence on the fuller organism. It is no longer revered as the sacred apex of human existence, but is seen in a much humbler role, as one aspect, one mode of expression, one characterizing function, in the full range of human possibilities.

As Romanticism suspected—Mary Shelley's *Frankenstein* is a case in point—the mind is capable of demonic excesses, just as the body is. Dostoevsky's brilliant novel *The Brothers Karamazov* depicted his astute appraisal of what happens to a man whose preference for the intellectual leads to imbalance in his way of seeing the world; Ivan eventually lapses into insanity, while his brother Dmitri, who errs on the sensual side, recovers his wholeness; and the devil, whom Ivan sees in his terrible visions, turns out to be Ivan's alter-ego, the product of his overactive mind. And the technology of war, from the Nazis to the Pentagon and the Kremlin, is a product of the same excessess on an international scale.

It is little wonder that those who oppose these excesses in our time often adopt the pose of anti-intellectualism, dropping out of society and its educational systems, denouncing traditional learning processes, and living with an apparent emphasis on immediacy and human feeling.

There is a crasser side to the sensuality revolution, of course, in which all human emotions and feelings eventually get channeled into some form of sexual expression. Skin flicks, group orgies, and such popular books as *The Sensuous Woman, The Sensuous Man,* and *The Sensuous Couple* are manifestations of this aspect of the revolution. "The new sexistentialism" is what Benjamin DeMott called it in an article in *Saturday Review*[1]—a glorious celebration of human sexual freedom in our time.

But every revolution is subject to its pornographers—opportunistic hucksters who ply the soft peripheries of the battle areas, scavenging for salable items that will turn a quick profit on a minimal investment—and this ought not to be allowed to throw us off the greater significance of the revolution itself. The truth is that *body* is becoming a new language for modern man. There is a new premium on sensual awareness, on feeling and perception, in the Western world. In the Church, it tends to seek sanctification on the basis that the body has spiritual possibilities, that it is the temple of the Holy Ghost, that the will of God is known more readily by the whole man, body and soul, and not by a mere single aspect of his being. In the world at large, however, it needs no such justification. The body *is.* Period. It has feelings, and they are important.

Thomas Hanna, a philosopher and critic, predicts that the greatest discoveries of the centruy ahead will be those having to do with the human body and its response to the world around it. "During the coming generations," he says,

human individuals will cease thinking of themselves as minds or spirits precisely to the degree that they begin discovering themselves in the immediacy of their somaticity. It is not my point that we *should* not consider the immediacy of our selfhood as mental or spiritual, but rather that we *shall* not do so: it is no less than a matter of mutational change. For millennia it has been of practical advantage for individuals of the human race to emphasize and place value upon that aspect of their behavior which they have called mental or spiritual; but what has now come to be discovered is that the so-termed mental and spiritual aspects of our bodily being are only one aspect of our human possibilites—and

1. "Dynamite Growing out of Their Skulls," July 10, 1971, pp. 21-25, 51.

an aspect which has, moreover, constrained men to remain in an unbalanced and peculiar stance toward their environing world.[2]

Man's mental and spiritual acts, says Hanna, will come to be seen
for what they are: mere *functions* of the individual, not summar-
ies or epitomes of his entire being. They will take their place along
with all the othe functions which have heretofore been held sub-
sidiary to them.

### The Wisdom of the Body

The artists were among the first to call our attention to it. D. H.
Lawrence wrote that we were at "the *cul-de-sac* of mind-con-
sciousness." That is, the centuries of rationalism since the Renais-
sance had carried the business of the mind about as far as it could
go until something happened to bring the rest of man's being up
with it.

Lawrence was one of the real prophets of sensual wisdom at a
time when it was unpopular with the Church and government and
just about everybody in authority. Relentlessly, in poem, prose,
and drama. he pursued the theme of the importance of listening
to the body.

The novel by which he is best known in this country, *Lady
Chatterley's Lover,* is an illustration of the doctrine he preached.
Sir Clifford Chatterley, Lady Chatterley's husband, is an invalid
living in a wheelchair. An industrialist, he represents for Lawrence
at least part of what is wrong with society: he is a man of very little
feeling, yet he has vast power and wealth and controls the lives
of many persons. His physical impotence appears to have been
compensated for by intellectual keenness; yet he is only partly a
man. Lady Chatterley's lover, on the other hand, is a whole man.
A gamekeeper, he reciprocates with his environment. Sensitive,

2. Thomas Hanna, *Bodies in Revolt* (New York: Holt, Rinehart & Winston,
1970), p. 37.

appreciative, generous, he lives openly, fully, and compassionately. Connie Chatterley's love for him is not at all a sordid thing; on the contrary, it is her act of opening to life, the way a blossom yields itself to the sun.

Man was not meant to become mere mind, Lawrence was saying. He was created to be whole, complete, full. Only when his mind is drawing upon the strength of the body and upon the entire repertory of sensual data is it truly fulfilling its function.

A Frenchman, Paul Valéry, unwittingly created a caricature of the man who does almost become mere mind. A young man at the time, Valéry was much enamoured of the sciences and of the potentialities of the human brain. Almost as an ideal portrait, he drew the character of Monsieur Teste, whose very name, Old French cognate of the word *tête,* meant "head." Teste was an extraordinarily developed mental genius. Like Valéry himself, he lived only to think. He had long ago abandoned the amenities of everyday speech—all the idle conversation with which ordinary persons fill the day—and preserved his energies for serious contemplation. His wife, a much more lovable human being, worshiped him and slaved to please him daily, though he treated her as if she hardly existed.

Years later, Valéry confessed that he realized then that he had drawn only the caricature of a man—that Teste was not even human in his scrupulosity for all things mental. Life was much more than Teste could understand. He was only a kind of machine —advanced and complicated, perhaps, but still a machine.

Samuel Beckett has more recently illustrated the fallacy of divorcing the mind from the body and a full life, in his little play *Krapp's Last Tape.* Krapp, whose cloacal-sounding name is surely intended, has lived for his mind. For years and years, he has recorded his thoughts and observations on tape. Now he sits at a table, listening as his past is unfolded. The irony is that he can no longer bear to listen to anything he ever believed or thought.

Every time the recorder is on the verge of revealing some ponderous statement, he hits the "Forward" control button and sends the reel speeding ahead. The one episode in his life which continues to attract him concerns a time when he was with a girl in a punt on the water somewhere. That, of all his memories and records, has significance to him. Time and again, he turns the tapes back to that single occurrence. It is the *physical* episode— the one having to do with his body—that continues to have meaning for him. All the rest has sunk into triviality or falseness. At the end of the play he has drunk too much, and his grizzled old face sinks to the table as the end of a tape flaps wildly on the revolving reel.

There is a reason for the artist's sensitivity in these matters. What he creates is, after all, the product of his whole being and puts demands upon every facet of his personality and character. Others may reduce or construct the amount of themselves that enters their work; it consists then principally of technique or method. But the artist must give freedom to everything in him, must allow it all to be and to get in. Mind is not enough for him. He must see, feel, create, with everything.

## The World We Almost Lost

The denial of the senses which was sanctioned jointly by asceticism, Puritanism, and rationalism has doubtless cost many persons their enjoyment of the world they have lived in. It is impossible to say how much its practice during earlier centuries has affected our own capacity for being fully present in the sensual environment.

At its worst, repression of the body leads to severe imbalance of the personality—even to extreme schizophrenia. The body is, after all, the only way we have of experiencing the reality of the world around us. If we refuse its authority, we are bound to suffer a sense of distortion and confusion. Our very sense of identity is thrown off, for it depends on some clear understanding of our relationship to the enrivonment.

Alexander Lowen, a medical doctor, writes in *The Betrayal of the Body* of the correlation between people's inability to draw symmetrical human bodies and their failure to grasp the reality of the world. Many persons have learned to despise their physical being so much—especially their sexual organs—that they simply cannot bring themselves to represent those parts of their bodies on paper. Their vision of the world, says Lowen, suffers a consequent distortion. They are prone to hallucination and perceptual misrecognition. Some become positively schizoid, with vacant stares that signal their complete separation from the world of external signification.

The phrase we use to describe such persons, "out of touch," is itself indicative of their condition. It speaks of their having lost their grip on reality because the transmitting agency, the body, is no longer functioning as a go-between, is no longer relational.

Scientists have conducted experiments in recent years to determine the effects of sensual deprivation or distortion on people. In one such experiment, volunteers were clothed in heavy, insulated clothing, thick gloves and socks, and distortion goggles. They were put into a soundproof cube suspended inside a closed room and asked to remain there without speaking as long as they could. Some could stay only a very brief time; others managed for several hours. All of them suffered perceptual distortion. One person's arm seemed so heavy that he walked bent to the side. Another complained that his head appeared to be spinning off into space. Several suffered from severe attacks of nausea.

The point is that the human body is our only contact with physical reality; in that sense it *is* our reality; and ignoring that fact or downgrading it inevitably detracts from our knowing either the world or ourselves.

Rudolf Arnheim, distinguished professor of psychology of art at Harvard University, says that our very culture and its educational system conspire to alienate us from the world we live in. Devising their own formulas and language, they turn us more and more from the real world to the house of mirrors they are making. They induce "perceptual pellagra" in us—the disease of sensory deficiency. We learn to manipulate figures and words that have lost their relationship to the world from which they were orignally derived. Everything acquires a kind of plastic or artificial nature.

"We are the victims," says Anheim, "of a tradition according to which our senses furnish nothing better or worse than the raw material of experience." Words, which enable us to name our experiences, become surrogates for the experiences themselves— mere "fossils of experience." We become experiential cripples, withdrawing more and more from real contact with the environment and dealing more and more in the symbols we devise to represent it.[3]

## The Quick Trip and the Long Way Back

Now there seems to be almost a rush to correct this situation. Everywhere we turn there are evidences of a massive return to sensuality. Sensitivity and awareness training, books and articles about sensuous living, an emphasis on aesthetics in city planning, engineering, and architecture, new attitudes toward sexuality and play—one would almost deduce that we are in a crash program to restore in a decade the relationships we have abused for generations and even centuries.

I have mentioned William Schutz of the Esalen Institute in California who says that what we must regain is a "bodymind concept"—a recognition of the total unity of the body and the mind that is itself so complete as to become part of the unconscious apparatus of our thinking. We are estranged from our bodies, he says, and cannot know anything as truth until we get back to them.

For this reason Schutz puts a premium on body exploration in

3. "Eyes Have They, but They See Not," Rudolf Arnheim in an interview with James R. Petersen, *Psychology Today* (June 1972), pp. 55 ff.

the encounter sessions he leads. "If I know what my body tells me," he says, "I know my deepest feelings and I can choose what to do."[4] Knowing the body requires attentiveness to it—really listening to it.

Schutz suggests this exercise, which he learned from a fellow therapist named Dorothy Nolte, as a beginning: Close your eyes and imagine that you wish very pointedly to be somewhere else. Yet someone is detaining you where you are. You want to go, but you cannot. Where do you feel this struggle physically?

Some persons will feel it in the arms, some in the back, some in the jaw, some in the stomach. Schutz says he experiences such things as a pull in the throat. The first time he became conscious of this, he thought back on his proneness to get sore throats. Sure enough, he could identify some of those occasions with times when he was in situations he found undesirable. Later, when he would begin getting a sore throat, he would analyze his present situation to articulate what was annoying him. He found that being able to flush the annoyance into the open usually made the sore throat go away.[5]

Ida Rolf, a physical therapist who is a colleague of Schutz, has developed a famous massage technique, called "Rolfing," which is based on a conflict theory of therapy. Briefly, the theory is that muscle tension is a way of stopping feeling—for example, we contract the muscles in our forearms when pain is inflicted on the wrist—and that chronic tension eventually results in cramped or constantly tight muscles. Rolf's technique, then, is to find the muscles in a person's body that are tight and unrelaxed, and to provide the kind of deep massage and exercise that will uncramp those muscles. Often dealing with the muscles themselves leads to a reencounter with the psychological situation that originally

4. William Schutz, *Here Comes Everybody* (New York: Harper & Row, 1971), p. 1.
5. *Ibid.*, pp. 2–10.

developed the muscular tightness, and the two things may be treated simultaneously, freeing the individual from this distortion in his personality.

Dealing with the body can be a theatening experience to mature persons who have become strangers to their physical selves. There is no doubt that a tremendous isolation of the mental and bodily functions has occurred in modern American life. Businessmen who sit behind corporate desks all day, housewives who emerge from their homes only to drive to the market, even young schoolchildren who spend many hours a day sitting in classrooms or watching television, lose the intimacy they once had with their limbs their breathing; their ingestion, digestion, and elimination processes; their walking, their sleeping—everything about their physical persons except their aches and pains and discomforts. Suddenly to be brought into conversation with the body again, after years of alienation from it, is like being confronted by an old friend one has abused. Yet there is a sense in which the fuller redemption of man lies through this single pathway, so that it can be reached in no other direction.

Bernard Gunther, another Esalenite, has developed numerous simple exercises for physical sensitivity which can be performed by individuals, couples, or even groups. Many of these are described in his books *Sense Relaxation Below Your Mind* and *What to Do Until the Messiah Comes.* They are designed to return persons to an awareness of the sights, sounds, and textures of the world, and of their feeling for these phenomena. For example, they include an exercise for savoring an orange: its feel, its roundness, its aroma, the feast of experience it affords when it is peeled and tasted.

If there appears to be a touch of Eastern mysticism in the sensitivity movement, there is good reason for it. Oriental religions have often, put a higher premium upon the senses than Judaism and Christianity. The latter have had a strong historical character, concerned with dynasties and epochs, The former, on the other hand, have shown great interest in the aesthetic, in the way the human eye beholds its surroundings.

Rudolf Arnheim has related a charming story of his encounter with this trait in Zen Buddhism. He had been given a teaching fellowship in Japan and had just arrived at a small monastery in the hills outside Kyoto.

One of the monks showed me around. We stopped in a tearoom that had the usual shoji screens, paper windows and paper walls. He opened one of them, slid it aside, and said "See out there." I looked and there was a small maple tree about 20 feet from the window. The monk continued, "In September when the leaves turn red, the reflection of the red leaves are going to show on this paper window. That will happen at a particular time every year, and it will be seen every year." When I heard that I caught a glimpse of something that was really thousands of years —or thousands of miles—away from the culture I had grown up in.[6]

Perhaps this is one reason the late Thomas Merton felt such an affinity for Zen: he found in it the same humanizing factors that were present in the monastic life he loved so dearly at Gethsemani, the little community in the hills of Kentucky. It advocated the life of contemplation and perception, and helped people to be in touch with themselves and the world.

Drugs have likewise had a certain association with the recent emphasis on bodily experience. Schutz is unequivocal on this matter: he thinks that tripping often helps people to get beyond their inner defenses and have significant encounters with themselves at levels of high productivity, so that they are later able to work through the difficulties they formerly had in handling certain problems or aspects of their personalities.[7]

6. From James R. Petersen, "The Beholder: A Sketch of Rudolf Arnheim," *Psychology Today* (June 1972), p. 59.
7. Op. cit., p. 13.

My own way of putting it is that drugs eradicate the artificial boundaries people have erected between their conscious and unconscious selves, permitting them to draw on their full potentials in experiencing the world and themselves. Chemicals produce for them what artists such as Chagall and Picasso live with constantly: a sense of freedom to let the world be what it is without editorializing or reconstructing it, and to represent their own inner response to it in the wildest, most imaginative way they wish. The artist trains himself to see and feel with his total being; or perhaps he never loses this ability from childhood. Drugs permit average individuals with all the perceptual hang-ups induced by society and its training to experience for a brief duration what the artist has as a perpetual way of being in the world.

In their *Varieties of Psychedelic Experience* R.E.L. Masters and Jean Houston have given numerous acounts of testimonies of drug users to the increased sensitivity they experienced on trips.[8] Generally there is a heightening of perceptivity for all sensual data.

I remember the description an off-Broadway playwright once gave me of one of his trips. His "guide," or person caring for him during the trip, put a Symanowski recording on the record player and placed a burning candle on the table where he could see it. "The music," sad the playwright, "entered my body and filled it, an though my body were a temple. It went into every part of me, even my toes and fingers. Somehow the music and the flame became one, and as the music diminished in intensity the flame would die down. Once, the music stopped—maybe the record had to be turned over—and the flame went out. I screamed in the darkness. Then the music began again, and the flame came back. My screaming turned to laughter. I was overjoyed. For days afterward when I walked in the street I was aware of the bricks in the buildings. I had never paid any attention to them before. But now

8. New York: Dell Publishing Co., 1966.

they were *there*—they were presetnt to me. Lots of little things were the same way. I felt kind toward all of them, toward everybody, toward the whole world."

In the past, salvation has often been regarded as redemption *from* the world. But an obvious reversal is occurring in our culture, and salvation more and more has to do with being saved *to* the world. How can I live before I die? What will put me in touch with reality again? Where is my childhood, now that I am older? I must find it, for it was real. The world was real then. Now there is so much illusion.

The words of Norman O' Brown gather up a widespread sentiment: "The last thing to be realized is the incarnation. . . . Christ, the fulfillment, is not an abstract idea but a human body. All fulfillment is carnal, *carnaliter adimpleri.*"[9]

For centuries we have been bent on trying to get beyond the world. We have drawn saints to resemble the El Grecoish, elongated figures in medieval monasteries, spindly cadavers whose very physiques suggest flames that leap upward, away from the sordidness of earthly existence. But now we are trying to return, trying to learn what the wise old Father Zossima advised, to "kiss the earth, and to love it with a fierce, consuming passion."

## The Dissenting Perspective

There is undoubtedly a kind of healthiness involved in redressing the imbalance between mind and body in our Western culture. It is almost as if the organism of mankind itself were attacking its point of illness, trying to throw off a disease that had almost reached the crippling stage for many of us. Keen *should* listen to the sun on his shoulders. In Puritanism and rationalism we fended off important aspects of our nature and environment. Now we

9. Norman O. Brown, *Love's Body* (New York: Vintage Books, 1966), pp. 221–22.

must learn again to live openly in communion with the realities that cradle our being.

Yet certain perennial problems of human existence—notably pain, illness, and death—are not answered by a new respect for physicality. Not entirely, at least. They may be altered somewhat, or viewed in a different light. But they are not completely dissipated.

I recall, for example, a recent conversation with a woman who is severely afflicted with crippling arthritis. Her hands are drawn into unwilling fists, and locomotion even with a crutch is agonizingly slow and painful.

Watching a child skip gracefully through the room, she observed, "I once ran like that. I could run like a deer. I was always running, wherever I went. I would race down to the mailbox every day to get the mail. I ran to the store with my money in my hand, and when I got there I was so breathless I couldn't tell them what I wanted."

There was something beautiful, yet sad, in the memory. It was such a contrast with her present condition, which forces her to sit in her room all day, emerging only for meals.

Knowing this person as I do, I suspect that her awareness of her body is not all negative. There is a playfulness about her that suggests a psychological distance betewen her personality and her affliction. Yet the tragedy of an immobile body will not go away —will, in fact, get worse. And it defies, finally and irrevocably, any mindless assertion that the body is all, that salvation is primarily physical.

We do not need to correct the imbalance. That is obvious. But an imbalance on the other side is no cure either.

Bodymind.

Not bodyMIND, and not BODYmind.

Bodymind.

# 7

# Jesus or Che?

Rosemary Ruether, in *The Radical Kingdom,* observes that apocalypticism, which is "the social religion of oppressed people," has become an important option in the world again since the collapse of the Church. During New Testament times it was the revolutionary spirit *par excellence,* promising a new world to the poor, the hungry, and the enslaved. Then it gradually lost its revolutionary character as it was absorbed by the age of the institutional Church. Religion, as Marx correctly said, became the opiate of the people. Now, with the death of the Church and its power to coopt apocalyptic sentiment, revolution has come into its own again with striking visions of a world where social problems are solved.

It would be difficult to imagine an age more characterized by social unrest than the one we now live in. Even the decades of the death of feudalism and the birth of the modern world witnessed fewer dislocations of life, property, and ideology. The incredible development of communications technology in this century, and particularly in the last thirty years, has made possible not only instant knowledge of any insurrectionary act but instant sympathy and duplication as well. Events in Zambia or Cambodia send

**129**

immediate tremors through the concrete canyons of Wall Street. An escalation of the bombing of North Vietnam draws thousands of students from communes and campuses to demonstrations and protest marches.

As Dean Peerman and Martin E. Marty said in the introduction to their *New Theology* volume on revolution two or three years ago, "One hesitates to begin the catalog of evidences because he cannot end it and one knows that after he lays down his pen and submits his writing for publication, many new events of revolt, rebellion, revolution—and certainly reaction and repression—will have begun to make his listings out of date." They could only, they confessed, introduce such evidences "as incantations and for liturgical effect" to register a single point—that the world to which theologians (they might have said *Christians*) address themselves "is not a world of subtle political shifts, quiet and respectful dialogue, or nuanced adjustments."[1]

Indeed it is not! It is a world of profound upheaval, of bombings, marches, *coups d'état,* assassinations, and city-burnings—a world, in James Baldwin's words, of "the fire next time"!

And there are millions of people in the world who expect to be saved by fire.

## Too Close for Comfort

It would be nice if we could discuss this incendiary matter with polite academic detachment, as though it were an African or European or Chinese phenomenon and had little to do with our lives in the United States. But this is far from the case.

As Jean-François Revel said in his widely read book *Without Marx or Jesus,* it is in the United States that the worldwide revolution has the best chance of succeeding.

---

1. Dean Peerman and Martin E. Marty, eds., *New Theology No. 6* (New York: The Macmillan Co., 1969), pp. 8–9.

There are five aspects of revolution which must occur simultaneously for the major revolution to succeed, said Revel: a political revolution, a social revolution, a technological and scientific revolution, a revolution in culture and values, and a revolution in international and interracial relations. And it is only in the United States that all five appear to be in progress at once and organically related to each other in such a way as to constitute a single revolution.

The "hot" issues in "America's insurrection against itself," as enumerated by Revel, are:

a radically new approach to moral values;
the black revolt;
the feminist attack on masculine domination;
the rejection by young people of exclusively economic and technical social goals;
the general adoption of noncoercive methods in education;
the acceptance of the guilt for poverty;
the growing demand for equality;
the rejection of an authoritarian culture in favor of a critical and diversified culture that is basically new, rather than adopted from the old cultural stockpile;
the rejection both of the spread of American power abroad and of foreign policy; and
a determination that the natural environment is more important than commercial profit.[2]

The important point, according to Revel, is that these issues, numerous and different as they are, form a coherent whole. None of the advocates of a single issue could have got the hearing each

2. Jean-François Revel, "Without Marx or Jesus," *Saturday Review,* July 24, 1971, p. 17.

has attained, apart from the impetus of all the others. Together they constitute one of the most massive attacks on a traditional system ever imagined.

It is no wonder that the average middle-aged American feels a sense of vertigo unmatched by his counterpart in older European nations. For years it was a cliché that Americans had no cultural history, that they were without roots in the past similar to those of native Europeans. Now many Europeans, I have found, regard this as a reason for the technological aggressiveness of the United States, an aggressiveness they see despoiling their own time-honored traditions and cultural ways. But they misunderstand. Many Americans are as bewildered by the rapid changes occurring in their world as are Europeans, perhaps even more so. As residents of an experimental country (that is, one whose very government is an experiment), they have less ballast to stabilize them.

Americans are likewise less accustomed to upheaval. Their geographical isolation has protected them from the ravages of constant wars and invasions. They have not experienced enemy fire on their own soil for more than a century and a half.

It is little wonder, therefore, that radio and television stations in the city of Detroit, during the riots there a few summers ago, were beseiged by callers inquiring whether it was safe to venture out of doors in their own neighborhoods; or that five out of ten university presidents selected by the government to be sent on a tour abroad had resigned their posts between the date of their selection and the time of the trip; or that horrified women delegates at a political dinner shrieked and ran from the room when two coeds serving the meal stripped and came forward bearing the heads of pigs on silver platters.

The average American, lulled by the propaganda that this is the "freest" and "most productive" nation in the history of the world, is not prepared for the signs of an apocalyptic revolution. It is too staggering for his imagination. He cannot believe it. It threatens his entire way of looking at the world.

## The Black Issue

Of the five aspects of revolution which Revel said must occur simultaneously if the total revolution is to succeed, four are in evidence together in several European nations. The one aspect that distinguishes the United States from most of them is the revolution in race relations.

It would be impossible to overestimate the significance of this particular element to the total spirit of the revolution in the United States today. Part of the reason for this significance is the way the history of the country has been intertwined with the roots of racial injustice. As Leslie Fiedler pointed out in *Waiting for the End,* the greatest literature written by American authors from Mark Twain to the present time has been primarily concerned with the relationship of the white man to the black man or the red man. Secretly, says Fiedler, every American male wants to be a black man, a red man, and a Jew; it is the dream that dominates our unconscious and expresses our guilt, a guilt we can never assuage.

The American Negro was a classic instance of the use of religion as a means of fantasy to relieve real revolutionary potential. When African slaves were first imported into America, they were regarded by white Christians as beasts or devils without souls. They were forbidden to practice their own cultic ways, but were given no instruction in Christian teachings. Later, when they were permitted to worship the white God and to have services of their own, these services became the primary inspiration they had, inculcating belief in a "hebben" with golden streets where even the darkies would be "white as snow."

As William Brink and Louis Harris observe in *The Negro Revolution in America,* the black man desperately needed such a religion:

It filled a great vacuum in his life of subjugation and despair. Denied any other kind of rights and considered by the whites to be subhuman, the Negro discovered in his church the only place where he could be a person. There he could at least find a brief surcease from slavery; there he could run his own affairs and worship as he pleased.[3]

Indeed, the special role of his own church in the black man's life had much to do with the highly emotional and physical characteristics of his worship that survive even today. The ring dances, shuffle dances, shouting, and clapping provided a release for pent-up feelings and produced a kind of ecstatic "deliverance" from the trials of earthly life.

It is small wonder, therefore, that the militant black youth of today speak contemptuously of the Christian Church as an instrument of bondage in the hands of white slave masters. In *We Own the Night,* a play by black author Jimmy Garrett, one of the characters calls God "the last dick the whiteman's got to put in you." And black poet Bobb Hamilton, in a poem entitled "Brother Harlem Bedford Watts Tells Mr. Charlie Where Its At," accuses the white man of having paid off some "rib picking Baptist Nigger preacher" to go around telling the black man to love him every time the white man kicks him.

The mother in Garrett's play, like the mammies in most black plays, opposes the revolutionary attitudes of her children. Hers is the Miltonic philosophy that insurrection is rebellion against God. Her son's is the outlook of Camus, that rebelling is sometimes the only positive act. He says: "He is your God and I have sworn to kill God. Can't you understand, Mama. We're gonna build a whole new thing after this. After we destroy the white man. Black people don't want to kill. We want to live. But we have to kill first. We have to kill in order to win."[4]

3. William Brink and Louis Harris, *The Negro Revolution in America* (New York: Clarion Books, 1963), p. 97.
4. Jimmy Garrett, *We Own the Night,* in LeRoi Jones and Larry Neal, eds., *Black Fire: An Anthology of Afro-American Writing* (New York: William Morrow & Co., 1968), p. 538.

The language is apocalpytic: "a whole new thing after this." The black vision is that of a new world where black is beautiful—not ugly; and powerful—not poor.

And violence seems a small price to pay for such a world. As Eldridge Cleaver said in *Soul on Ice*, "We shall have our manhood. We shall have it or the earth will be leveled by our attempts to gain it."[5]

Calvin C. Hernton made the same point in an article in *Boss* magazine. He told of going as a welfare worker to the apartment of an unwed mother in Harlem. On one of the walls, drawn by her twelve-year-old son, was a picture of black people being beaten by men in blue uniforms. Standing by and watching, with wads of money falling out of their pockets, were white men. One of them was saying, "You niggers love us, don' you." Hernton noticed that the hair of all the blacks was standing up in plaited tips, and that there was blood on the tips. When he commented on the blood, the mother corrected him. "That's not hair with blood on it," she said, "that's dynamite growing out of their skulls."[6]

## Sharper than a Serpent's Tooth

In retrospect, the youth revolt in this country appears to have begun in the civil rights movement. College students especially, their sense of justice honed to a fine edge, converged on Alabama and Washington, D.C. to join their black brothers and sisters in protest against a system which was obviously prejudicial and unfair to Afro-Americans.

Then the blacks told the students to go home, they didn't want them any more. This was a black thing and blacks would do it for themselves. White youths were stymied. They found themselves

5. Eldridge Cleaver, *Soul on Ice* (New York: Dell Publishing Co., 1968), p. 61.
6. Jones and Neal, eds., op. cit., pp. 101–102.

uninvited to a party they had helped to start. For a while it appeared that they had no cause—that they might as well return to their campuses and do business as usual.

But then the idea was born that the student himself was a kind of nigger. The phrase "the student as nigger" made the rounds of the campuses. Overnight a new protest movement emerged. First it hit Berkeley, which was ripe because the university there had grown so quickly and haphazardly that not even some of the officials were familiar with channels of authority. Students complained that they were only numbers in the university, presided over and programed by a computer. They demanded rights as citizens—free speech and assembly being among them. But the speech was liberally peppered with four-letter words and the assemblies were so large that police couldn't handle them. The university resisted. The fracas grew. Soon it had popped out all over the country—in Michigan, Ohio, New York, Massachusetts —and a whole new phase of the revolution was under way!

Charles Reich says it marked the emergence of a new consciousness—the third consciousness—in America. Consciousness I he defines in terms of the founding fathers and pioneers who built the country; they were serious, hard-working, and dedicated to the idea that godliness and perseverance are the central virtues of man. Consciousness II Reich views as the corporate sensibility; in general it still accepts the ideas of Consciousness I, but modifies them to the needs of the political state and technicalization. Consciousness III, although it grows out of I and II, challenges their assumptions and asks whether the good life they envision is really good.

"The new consciousness," says Reich, "is the product of two interacting forces: the promise of life that is made to young Americans by all of our affluence, technology, liberation, and ideals, and the threat to that promise posed by everything from neon ugliness and boring jobs to the Vietnam War and the shadow of nuclear holocaust."[7]

In some ways, this revolution in American life has been harder for the average citizen to understand than the black revolution. He feels that he has loved his children and has worked hard to provide for them. He even fought a war for them. Guadal canal, Anzio, Manila—it was all to make the world safe for democracy and for the generation yet unborn. Therefore he feels somehow betrayed when his sons refuse to fight another war of containment, when his sons and daughters sit in the university president's office instead of in the classroom, when they cohabit in the dormitories, when they turn on with drugs and let their hair grow and refuse to conform to "the American way of life."

This is perhaps the first time a successful revolution has been mounted against a system in which the rebels themselves were for the most part well-fed, well-clothed, well-housed, and wellheeled. Usually poverty, hunger, or oppression has been necessary as the basis for such a movement. But the young say that ideological repression is a greater evil than all the others. They accuse their parents of being blind to the major cancers of their society, and tuning in and dropping out is the only way to dramatize these cancers and perform the necessary operation on them.

The technique of counterculture which the younger generation has developed as an antidote to the cancerous mainline culture has proven immensely effective. For the most part it has been nonviolent. Its textbooks may include Marx, Mao, and Marcuse, but they also include Breton and Artaud, the pioneers in surrealism and the absurd. The surrealist saw that it was hopeless to try to mount a major cultural assault on the status quo using its own weapons; what was required was a radically subversive tactic, a

7. Charles A. Reich, *The Greening of America* (New York: Bantam Books, 1971), p. 234.

way of undercutting old visions of reality with dreams and fantasies, of pelting machine gunners with flowers and olive pits.

Abbie Hoffman, in *Revolution for the Hell of It*, relates two of the choicer tactics used by his group during the early years of the revolution. One was the attempt, at the Democratic convention in Chicago, to enter a pig on the balloting for the presidential nomination. The other was the rite for exorcising the Pentagon. Guards found a bunch of young people trying to measure the sides of the Pentagon with a tape. They explained that they were preparing to levitate the building by repeating an Oriental chant, but first needed to take its exact dimensions. When it was in the air, they would make it revolve and spin out all the evil spirits.

Expecting the guards to be armed with mace, Hoffman's group called a press conference prior to the exorcism attempt to announce that they had developed a new chemical called "lace" which would be used in the counterwarfare. Lace, they explained, was a special aphrodisiac in the form of purple foam; when sprayed on a victim, the victim felt an overwhelming desire to take off all his clothes and make love. The new chemical was then demonstrated in the reporters' presence. It was sprayed on two couples sitting on a couch; they immediately went into a trance-like state, removed their clothes, and began to make love.

Such shenanigans have undoubtedly altered public consciousness about the war and other major issues. The rebellion which was at first compared to old schoolboy japes of swallowing goldfish and cramming into telephone booths has become a powerful way of opposing the traditional culture. It is clear now that the refusal of the young to duel with their elders in merely verbal or logical encounters was strategically brilliant. As Jerry Rubin says in *Do It!*, his controversial report on the revolution, language actually *prevents* communication. The bastardization of such words as "love" and "adore" to apply to perfumes, deodorants, and gasolines has rendered them meaningless when applied to human beings. The four-letter Anglo-Saxonism for sexual inter-course, says Rubin, is the one remaining word in the English language and has therefore become a kind of symbol to the youthful revolutionary. In the end, the revolution had to transcend verbal argument. There the older generation always held the upper ground. Turning on and dropping out was the only way.

It is difficult to say how completely young rebels are taken in by their own words and antics and really believe that a kind of salvation lies ahead through their brand of take-over. Some are probably naïve enough to believe it totally, others cynical enough to disbelieve it just as totally. But there is an aura of apocalypse in much of the language used, whether the hope is genuine or not.

Hoffman, for example, describes a great march on Washington this way:

Yahoo! We will dye the Potomac red, burn the cherry trees, panhandle embassies, attack with water pistols, marbles, bubble gum wrappers, bazookas, girls will run naked and piss on the Pentagon walls, sorcerers, swamis, witches, voodoo, warlocks, medicine men, and speed freaks will hurl their magic at the faded brown walls. Rock bands will bomb out with "Joshua fit the Battle of Jericho." We will dance and sing and chant the mighty OM. We will fuck on the grass and beat ourselves against the doors. Everyone will scream "VOTE FOR ME." We shall raise the flag of nothingness over the Pentagon and a mighty cheer of liberation will echo through the land. "We are Free, Great God Almighty, Free at last." Schoolchildren will rip out their desks and throw ink at stunned instructors, office secretaries will disrobe and run into the streets, newsboys will rip up their newspapers and sit on the curbstones masturbating, storekeepers will throw open their doors making everything free, accountants will all collapse in one mighty heart attack, soldiers will throw down their guns. "The War is over. Let's get some ass." No permits, no N.Y. *Times* ads, no mailing lists, no meetings. It will happen because the time is ripe. Come to the Day of Judgment.[8]

8. Abbie Hoffman, *Revolution for the Hell of It* (New York: Pocket Books, 1970), pp. 43–44.

### Can Revolution Ever Succeed?

We are haunted in all these revolutionary hopes by one sobering truth: no revolution has ever been permanently successful. As Hannah Arendt says in *On Revolution,* liberation and freedom are not the same thing; the one may be produced by revolution, but the other is guaranteed by nothing. Liberation from one form of slavery is often followed by another kind of subjugation.

This is particularly noticeable in revolutions of state, such as those in Russia and China. But it is probably just as true in cultural and philosophical revolutions.

Genêt has given us the parable in his play *The Balcony.* While a revolution is going on in the streets and underground, the patrons of a bordello called The Balcony are blithely pursuing their fantasies of sex and power. One man is acting out his desire to be a bishop; another is playing the part of a judge; a third is accoutered as a general. They are all enjoying the pleasures for which such houses are noted.

The revolutionaries outside succeed in assassinating the queen and her first ministers. There is fear that the populace will rise up in anarchy and destroy everything, so the false bishop, judge, and general are fetched from the bordello, along with the madame, to take the place of their real counterparts. The populace is unable to tell the difference, and the impostors elect to continue in their parts indefinitely. All except the madame, that is—she alone is without illusions, being mistress of a house of illusions, and chooses to return to her former position.

The most telling commentary on revolutions, however, occurs when the young revolutionaries themselves take over positions of power and authority in the government they have toppled. One young man in particular has secretly coveted the place of chief of police. He usurps the chief's position, identifies it with sexual command, and has himself immured in a gignatic replica of a phallus.

Theodore Roszak, in *The Making of a Counter Culture,* expresses fears that a similar fate will finally overtake the black revolution. He sees the blacks as engaged primarily in a crusade to get what the whites already have. He understands also the power of any system for coopting the energy of a movement which covets its rewards and simply seeks to displace the present holders of them. The blacks will lean hard on the door of the system, he predicts; then suddenly the door will open and they will come tumbling in like slapstick characters in an old movie. Once inside, their power to alter the system itself will be gone. They will have lost the perspective from which the system might have been criticized and changed.

This may be one reason for placing more hope in the youth revolution, for it has come out of the system itself and constitutes at least a partial rejection of the system. The tactics of subversion by humor and absurdity may also lend an attitude of self-criticism to the youth movement that is missing from both the black and Third World revolutions. They must be serious; they are the revolutions of have-nots trying to conquer the haves and to become haves. But the young people who are making war on the old America are already haves in many cases; they will not be beguiled by the system the way the have-nots are. What they seek is to amend the system itself, to purge it of its hypocrisies and redirect it to its altruistic goals, and to correct it, now that the technetronic society is in view, from its aim of becoming a mere society of plenty.

**The Heroes of the Revolution**

Although American youth are after something essentially or qualitatively different from what blacks and Third World revolutionaries are after, they have readily identified with freedom movements all over the world. They have responded with a sense of immediacy to McLuhan's notion of a "global village" and have seen, perhaps better than their elders, the necessity of what might be called cosmoptic point of view.

They have consequently identified with an unusual array of "heroes" among the emerging or mutating nations of the world. Their strange pantheon includes such figures as Mao, Ho Chi Minh, Castro, Rap Brown, Eldridge Cleaver, Che Guevara, and General Giap—all names to redden the necks of old-fashioned defenders of American ideals.

José Míguez-Bonino, President of Union Theological Seminary in Buenos Aires, cites the case of an eleven-year-old child of Protestant parents who was asked to give the name of the first person to occur to him on hearing certain words. The child reacted as follows:

Death: "Jesus."

Liberation: "Che."[9]

In the face of this, it is hardly to be wondered that the youth culture has likewise come up with its own Superstar version of the person of Jesus. To many young people today (those in the Jesus Movement are probably exceptions) he is no longer the mysteriously transcendent Messiah or Christ, but a winsome human figure struggling with the notion of revolution and human liberation. They can dig this kind of Jesus, as they say. They feel his vibes.

It is perhaps another case of which came first, the chicken or the egg, but the whole liberation context of our time is witnessing a review of the Jesus question by professional scholars and theologians which is producing a reassessment of him as a possible revolutionary. Bishop Pike, whose intuitions were often on target

9. José Míguez-Bonino, "Theology and Liberation," *International Review of Missions* (January 1972), p. 66.

even when his judgment was poor, before his death produced numerous notes which his widow subsequently shaped into a volume called *The Wilderness Revolt,* in which the late bishop wondered with come cogency about Jesus's connections with the Zealots, a band of revolutionary Jews dedicated to the overthrow of the Roman occupation.

Dale Brown, a scholar and a less flamboyant figure than Pike, assesses the matter thus:

> Whether one accepts the presuppositions of a revolutionary hermeneutic or not, it will be necessary to be in conversation with the exegetical conclusions. For current reflections on many biblical themes focus on the revolutionary nature of the gospel. It is maintained that in the biblical tradition the name for God is revolutionary. *Yahweh* is devived from a root suggesting "to become or to come to pass." The doctrine of creation out of nothing points to a dynamic revolutionary perspective which is change-oriented rather than preservation-oriented. The prophetic theme of promise and fulfillment does not depict the movement of history so much in terms of a neat evolutionary course as in terms of judgment and tearing down, salvation and building up. The central Exodus motif is one of a deliverance from political enslavement and the sending forth of a pilgrim people into a new history.
>
> With the coming of Christianity we have the proclamation of the New Testament or covenant, the new Israel, the new man, the new wine, a new song, the new Jerusalem, a new heaven and earth, and the promise: "Behold I make all things new" (Rev. 21:5). The doctrine of repentance indicates that the Christian life begins in crisis. The biblical concepts of rebirth, new life, and conversion point to a fundamental change—from sin to grace, from selfishness to love. The doctrine of conversion applied to all of life may well lead to a theology of revolution. The cross discloses that reconciliation is impossible apart from suffering. Death and resurrection, the death of the old and the birth of the new, is a basic revolutionary motif, perhaps more existentially understood by many pagan participants in the struggles of our time than by respectable members in the fold. Apocalypticism, messianism, and eschatology are being revived and

reinterpreted by biblical scholars in such a way as to bring the future into the present as a dynamic, living, political reality. In the theological halls of ivy there is a new marriage between eschatology and ethics. Christian social ethics now depicts the Christian life style as more radical and revolutionary than did the neoorthodox era of greater ambiguities and so-called biblical realism.[10]

What is happening, apparently, is that the work of God in Moses and Jesus is being rediscovered for our time through the idiom of our time, which is a revolutionary idiom. Thus people who could never have appropriated the biblical materials in a neoorthodox frame of reference are able to respond positively and enthusiastically to the theology of such writers as Jürgen Moltmann and Wolfgang Pannenberg, who emphasize the gritty reality of the sufferings of Jesus and the "protest character" of Christian faith in general.

Nor is it strange, under such circumstances, that Marx and Jesus should have come to be regarded as bedfellows, when for years and years we have been propagandized to view them as holding radically antithetical positions on all important subjects.[11] Moltmann, for example speaks very appreciatively of the young Marx's attempt to analyze the way in which religion uses "a perverted consciousness of the world" to divert men from historical realities and the possibility of revolution.[12] Marx did not hope for a regimented society dedicated to production and control; he

10. Dale W. Brown, *The Christian Revolutionary* (Grand Rapids, Mich.: William B. Eerdmans Co., 1971), pp. 21–22.
11. One of the frequently used evangelical stories of the past half-century has been one which purports to contrast the intentions of Marxism with those of Christianity. A Marxist is depicted standing on a soapbox making an appeal for conversions to his secular religion. Spying a shabbily outfitted man standing in the crowd, he points to him and declares, "Communism will put a new coat on that man!" Alas for him, there is also a Christian in the crowd (male, Caucasian, strongly evangelical) who sets the record straight. "Hold on!" cries out the Christian. "Christianity will put a new man in that coat!"
12. Cf. Jürgen Moltmann, "Toward a Political Hermeneutics of the Gospel," in Peerman and Marty, eds., op. cit., pp. 66–90.

would have been appalled at the present-day Russian version of the communist dream. He was concerned, instead, for the manner in which industrialization and the modern state acted to dehumanize individuals, and for discovering the means whereby man might more fully approximate his own humanity. If he was opposed to Christianity and designated it an opiate, it was because the Christianity he saw practiced in the world was egregiously allied to self-aggrandizing socioeconomic and political motivations.

The real "hero" of the revolution is Man himself, which may explain why there is such a confusion of hero images among the rebels, cutting across old lines of difference. The penultimate heroes—Mao, Che, Jesus—are antiheroes, little chaps, all struggling to bring in the age of the final hero.

Such a viewpoint ought not to occasion Christians great difficulty when they recall that Jesus's own designation for himself was the Aramaic title *barnasha,* which meant "the Man." Uncontestably, it was the ideal of humanity realized in Jesus the Man that has made the higher dimensions of the present revolution possible. Without his life and teachings, and especially without his altruistic death, the kind of commitments which foster and sustain the revolutionary spirit today might not even be thinkable.

## Can the Church Go Through the Eye of the Needle?

Whatever our reservations about the ultimate success or failure of revolutions in general, we can hardly resist affirming such affinities as exist between the Christian theology of history and current revolutionary hopes. But the question is harder than this. Can the Church itself, institutionally entangled and entrenched as it is, actually undergo revolution? Can its leaders and preachers bring themselves to subject it to a harrowing reformation in this age? Or will the Church as we have known it refuse the rehistoricizing of religion and eventually find itself left behind as mankind enters a new era?

The problem is stated succinctly by Neil Middleton, a Catholic writer: "The ways of thinking, the social patterns, the magisterial forms, the very nerves of christianity are all inseparable from the body of western society. The corruption of the church is the corruption of the west."[13] Yet the Church has from its inception been involved in the imagery and symbolism by which revolution is conceivable. Both Church and world stand in desperate need of the revolution; they must undergo it together. Institutional Christianity has not only accepted the propaganda of the Western way of life; it helped to create that propaganda. Now they must be purged together.

But how will the Church fare in such a shaking down? Prelates and lay leaders alike are understandably threatened. If the Kingdom of God judges the kingdom or kingdoms of the Church, the encounter will be as drastic as the one that formed the Church in the beginning, when John the Baptist and Jesus came preaching the terrible Good News of God against institutional Judaism.

Christians naturally tend therefore to shrink from such a confrontation. As Colin Morris observes in *Unyoung, Uncolored, Unpoor,* they will do anything—even reform the Church—to avoid it. It is not the popes and bishops and Church presidents who will prevent the revolution's reaching the Church, says Morris, or even the bourgeoisie who feel insecure if the altar furniture is rearranged. Neither of these could really stop a revolution that was occurring in earnest. Instead, it is the reformers themselves who prevent revolution. They recast things just enough to satisfy the demands of a radical future or an impending crisis, and the Church gets by a while longer.

13. Neil Middleton, *The Language of Christian Revolution* (London: Sheed & Ward, 1968), p. 166.

Morris, who was a missionary to Zambia, confesses that he favors violence, if necessary, to accomplish the revolution that is needed for the renewal of the human spirit in our time. The young, the colored, and the poor, he says, will have a hard time wresting any control of their destinies away from the old, the white, and the rich without it. The latter are cunning, and they have the system on their side.

To protect their interests, wars are engineered, dictators made and broken, governments bought and sold, currencies adjusted, and markets rigged. They preside over a vast Aladdin's cave into which a ragged world brings its treasure and where fewer and fewer get more and more. They are unbeatable because they make the rules. Even your cry of outrage is rendered meaningless because they own the very language you use. As they leave your mouth, your words are twisted and molded so that your abuse rings out like a hallelujah to their benevolence. Freedom is what *they* mean by freedom, democracy is what *they* mean by democracy, and they have the power to make *their* definitions stick. Pour forth your blazing revolutionary writings and they will oblige you by printing, publishing, and serializing them in their glossy Sunday newspapers. Then they'll bank the profits and laugh all the way home to Hampstead.[14]

They are the "Up-people," says Morris; and "Up-people" are never down. Even war is little more than a device by which they redistribute their wealth and revitalize their economies.

How can the Church really attack the Up-people? It exists in public favor by their decree. It includes them on its honor roll of members and contributors. An attack on them is an attack on itself. It depends on their largesse. And, as Robert McAfee Brown once said, nobody calls for a new deal when he has four aces in his hand!

Morris is convinced that Jesus was a true revolutionary. He was

14. Colin Morris, *Unyoung, Uncolored, Unpoor* (New York: Abingdon Press, 1969), p. 32.

young, colored, and poor in a country where these were the marks of the oppressed. Morris does not insist that Jesus was an active insurrectionist; but he reads him as one whose teachings of mercy and humanity aligned him with radically rebellious positions. The Church, he implies, is pusillanimous and fainthearted by comparison; it is unwilling to follow its Master to the death for what it says it believes.

He tells the Zambians that there is "little really gritty Christian thinking on revolution" to guide them:

You'll have to turn to the Marxists for that. In the interests of keeping a whole skin, you would do well to study the writings of Ho Chi Minh, Che Guevara, and Regis Debray. There *are* World Council of Churches documents on revolution which discuss Biblical Messianism, the Dynamics of Revolutionary Process, and the Augustinian View of Social Change (I am quoting from the subheadings of one) but don't tell you to keep your feet dry, your rifle clean; when to fight and when to run like hell. So they are of limited value.[15]

The days of the Christian earth-shakers, he is afraid, are gone. The old cry of the Thomas Müntzers—"The world will suffer a big jolt and the down-trodden shall arise!"—is heard only as a faint echo in the Church.

The polemicism of Morris's style should not turn us away from the truth of what he is saying. For every cultured despiser of religion in the world, there are surely two despisers of cultured religion. The Church *is* profoundly, perhaps inextricably, interrelated to the society in which it has thriven. And it may be time to destroy that Church, or at least to knock its walls down, so that the winds of apocalypse blowing in the world at large may sweep across the sanctuary too.

I shall never forget the story that was related to me by a priest who attended a conference of bishops in Paris. They were debat-

15. Ibid., p. 30.

ing a revision of the geometrical shape of the little cloth used in the Mass to cover the chalice. There was a great deal of noise in the street outside, and one of the bishops finally rose from the table and pulled in the wooden shutters on the windows. The noise, said the priest, was from the student riots of May 1968!

This picture, of a bishops' council debating a trifling matter while the new world was coming into being outside, has become a kind of template I hold up to the Church to judge it. Whenever it conforms to the pattern, I know that it understands nothing of its apocalyptic dimension.

Only as that dimension is recaptured can the Church become the Church of Jesus Christ. Only as it learns to be a pilgrim Church again—a Church with an empty pouch, traveling light, making great journeys before dawn—will the Church recognize the presence of the Master in its midst, and touched by that presence, once more turn the world upside down.

"One has to try," said Camus, "to do what Christianity never did: be concerned with the damned."

"Never" is not quite right; but the idea is sound.

# 8

# To the Future with Love

In Pär Lagerkvist's novel *Barabbas,* set in the time of Jesus, there is a harelipped woman who sleeps with society's outcasts in the ugly little valley of Ge-Hinnom, outside the city of Jerusalem. Waiting for the coming of sleep, she listens to the night sounds' the groanings of the old and the sick on their makeshift pallets and the tinkle of a leper's bells—the one who sometimes gets up and walks around because of the pain.

She thinks about Jesus and the Kingdom he is always talking about. "Tommorow at sunrise . . . Tomorrow at sunrise. . . . " It is a strange thought! Soon all the sick will be well and the hungry will be fed and there will be no more pain and loneliness.

Perhaps, she imagines, angels will swoop down and cover the entire valley with white canopies, and then spread great feasts upon them for the people.

Later in the story, when Jesus has been killed, an oppression of his followers is carried out. The woman with the harelip is sentenced and led to a stoning-pit that lies a little south of the city.

The pit is full of stones, which at the bottom are dark with old blood. A crowd of yelling people surrounds it. The woman is led down onto the stones. She stands helplessly in the middle as new

**150**

stones rain down upon her. She staggers forward a step or two with outstretched hands, crying out: "He has come! He has come! I see him? I see him!"

Then she falls to her knees, and as if seizing the hem of someone's garment clutches the air and says, "Lord, how can I witness for thee? Forgive me, forgive. . . ." Her body slumps on the stones, lifeless.

One is prompted to ask at this point what has happened to the Kingdom she expected.

Has she been betrayed?

Or did she find the Kingdom?

**The Kingdom Forever Coming**

"Thy kingdom come," Jesus said we were to pray.

And we mark the same disparity in our lives that we see in the harelipped woman's: the Kingdom has come, but not yet. It has come, but it is still coming.

Something has happened—life is not the same—but it is not all consummated.

We are easily confused.

In some ways, the Kingdom has come. To say that it has not is to ignore obvious manifestations of it—"conversions" and churches around the world—a healing ministry now represented by thousands of hospitals and medical units—welfare organizations concerned for the poor—the promise of prison reform—homes for the orphaned and the aged—a high view of humanity—two thousand years "stained by his blood," as Yeats put it.

But in other ways it is always ahead of us, beyond us, coming, and we wait, like Godot's tramps.

It is the waiting that bothers us—the fact that it has been nearly two thousands years, and the end is no nearer now than it was in the beginning. Was he wrong? We can't help asking. He meant well, but suppose he was mistaken. If he was—even a little, even a hair's breadth—should we follow him?

Yes. I am convinced that we should.

I have tried to defect—but his shadow is too long. Maybe it reaches through the ages until it renders the size of the man casting it absurd. Yet it is there. And it is the shape of the future. It has to be. There is no getting away from it.

I remember how I felt when I came away from seeing *The Last Picture Show*. It was my own adolescence I had watched on the screen, my own growing pains, my own home town—a home town imploded with passion begging for sublimation, for a way out.

"Christ—"I said, "they need Christ. Not the denuded Jesus of the scholars, but the Christ of our dreams, the Christ we have made of him, the Christ of the ages!"

This Christ was the shadow-Christ—the transhistorical Christ who gathers up all human hope—whether Jesus expected it or not.

I had felt a similar emotion after seeing *The Pawnbroker* several years before. All that suffering. First Nazerman's in the concentration camp, where he lost his wife and children. Then the hurt and loneliness of all those people who came into his shop in Harlem to pawn things that were dear to them. And finally that of Jesus Ortiz, who wanted to be the pawnbroker's son but was rejected. When Jesus stepped in the line of fire and was killed defending the old man, it did something to the latter. It shattered the wall he had built around himself. He went back into the shop from the sidewalk, where he had been holding the dead boy's head, and plunged his hand down on a paperspike.

I have never been so electrified. I came out of the theater knowing I had seen a vision. Not an ordinary vision, but *the* vision —what life is about! And I knew it is about Christ. I know it now, just thinking back on that moment.

"There are times," said Roethke, "when reality comes closer."

**History and Hope**

The problem is to reconcile the vision and what we know about human history—or what we think we know. Becoming acquainted with biblical criticism (how the books of the Bible were written, how they contradict each other, how they were shaped by a particular but by no means necessary view of the world, etc.) and with the vagaries of Church history, is a disillusioning experience. The more honestly realistic we become, the more clarified our dilemma: Christ or history. For the Christ of the naïve preacher is largely the product of history—a fabrication of well-intentioned but often mistaken understandings. And the quest to get back to the original, to the flesh-and-blood Jewish prophet who really expected the end of the world in his lifetime or shortly thereafter, is fraught with hardship and heartache. For some, it is like the business of defoliating an onion in search of the center—it is so small, when finally arrived at, as to have been hardly worth the trouble. Barth said once that Christ was only a point, an intersection of lines with no real dimensions at all—that he was a crater where an explosion had taken place, but with no debris or deposit left behind. But that is so disappointing to our human expectancies.

The theology of the last hundred years or more has been largely preoccupied with this dilemma. And though it was an unavoidable part of our coming of age, of entering the modern world, its impact on the Church has in most instances been shattering. It has left many of the laity and clergy as well deeply suspicious of theological education in general. They view the seminaries, especially the more liberal ones, as warrens of heretics, where otherwise enthusiastic and faithful young ministers are ruined in two or three years' time. Sectarian ministers often announce with pride that they have *not* been to seminary, and would not at the peril of their souls!

Only recently I sat by a businessman on a plane trip who asked about the divinity school where I am a professor. "Does anybody at that school *believe* anything?" he said. He told of a recent board meeting of his church, in the same city as the school, at which an extremely conservative minister had made a speech against the church's hiring any associates or interns who attend the school, on the grounds that if they had any religion when they entered its program they would soon lose it.

I patiently explained to the man what it is like for a young minister to go to seminary and struggle with the problem of Christ and history. "Imagine," I said, "that you have committed your life to being a minister in the name of the Christ who was preached to you from some evangelical pulpit. You have read the Bible, and maybe even some general books on religion and theology. Then you come to seminary and discover, in biblical classes, that the Gospel of John couldn't possibly have been written by a disciple of Jesus—all the textual evidences argue for its being of later origin, around the turn of the century. You find out that the Gospel of Matthew was 'slanted' for a Jewish audience and the Gospel of Luke for a Gentile audience. You learn, in history classes, that the important creeds and beliefs of the Church from the second century to the present were all the results of compromises and environmental situations."

The man blinked.

"Think how you would feel," I said. "You might be confused, or hurt, or both. You might be bullheaded and say, 'I'm going to believe what I want to, and the evidences be damned!' But, on the other hand, you might feel subdued and chastened, and go into a church afterward with considerable hesitation. You might even wonder if your original commitment hadn't come in a moment of emotional fervor when you really didn't have enough information at your disposal to make a sound judgment."

The man studied my remarks, then said, "Why don't the

schools send men like you around to explain all this to the churches?"

I had to admit it was a plausible idea.

But theology may be entering a new phase on the other side of the wasteland we have been through. Another way of speaking has come into the picture. Instead of focusing on the dilemma in the past—on the lengthened shadow of Jesus the apocalyptic Jew —it talks about the future and how the future "calls out" the past and the present. It has matured beyond the point of choking on the evidences for how the gospel has been changed through the ages and concentrates instead on how certain emphases in the early gospel are still dependable guides for struggling with and giving shape—human shape—to a future that holds both threat and promise.

The language of Friedrich Gogarten is instructive. He speaks of God as "the coming one," "the beyond in our midst," or "the future present with us." God is the eschatological being, the one who stands at the end of the way and draws us on until history is finally consummated in him.

The shift is radical. Instead of looking back and saying "He didn't come," we look forward and ask "When is he coming?" Instead of regarding Christ retrospectively and pondering his mistakenness, we take a place at his side and become sensitive to the ways in which even now the Kingdom is bursting in upon our earthly existence. The future probes us and keeps us open. It shatters our idolatries and makes us vigilant. It renews our hope and makes it possible to work again. History is not conflated or overlooked; it is put back into perspective, where faith overcomes it.

The ministers coming out of seminaries in the next twenty years, after studying Gogarten and Moltmann and Pannenberg, will not be like those of the past twenty years. They may make their laymen uneasy, for they will be more committed to aligning the churches with future-oriented programs in the world than to talking about scholastic theology and inward-looking ethics. But there will be a new glint of certainty in their eyes and a fresh sense of direction in their preaching and activities. Like Martin Luther King, Jr. and the Berrigan brothers, they will know what they have to do to serve the God of Jesus. Introspection is already giving way to action!

People who are overly concerned about whether Jesus's Messianic expectations were right or wrong, fulfilled or unfulfilled, will be left behind. A routed army is regrouping around his hopes for mankind and his dream of a transformed earth. It may not march like the Church Triumphant of the Middle Ages, in columns and platoons and flanking movements (some say this is an age for guerrilla warfare), but its spirit is triumphant, for it is sure of the future!

## Participation in God

Jürgen Moltmann is among those for whom this new perspective, scanning centuries beyond ours as well as behind it, liberates the spirit of Jesus to a new effectiveness in the present. The Church's emphasis on an afterlife and a doctrine of Last Things, he says, has resulted in a sterilizing of its potency in the world at hand; Messianic hope has thus been forced to erupt in secularized forms, bypassing the Church and its preaching. Moltmann's call, therefore, is for the Church to return to a faithful position on the gospel of eschatology.

From first to last [he says], and not merely in the epilogue, Christianity is eschatology, is hope, forward looking and forward moving, and therefore also revolutionizing and transforming the present. The eschatological is not one element *of* Christianity, but is the medium of Christian faith as such, the key in which everything in it is set, the glow that suffuses everything here in the dawn of an expected new day, For Christian faith lives from the raising of the crucified Christ, and strains after the promises of the universal future of Christ. Eschatology is the passionate suffering and passionate longing kindled by the Messiah. Hence eschatology cannot really be only a part of Christian doctrine. Rather, the eschatological outlook is characteristic of all Christian proclamation, of every Christian existence and of the whole Church.[1]

Marx was right, says Moltmann, to criticize Feuerbach's attempt to enlighten the "essence of Christianity," insisting instead on a new *historical realization* of religion. The "character of Protest" is central to the Messianic faith of Christianity: it enters into struggle with the way things are on earth, calling them into question and announcing the wrath of God on them.

God's wrath is not felt, however, as a future judgment awaiting some vaguely distant Last Day. On the contrary, it is immediate and stinging in its rebuke, working at once to transform the present situation. Jesus, because of his Jewish background and conditioning, expected a cosmological *coup* to topple the present structures and usher in the transformed society. But we must not gulp at this, says Moltmann; it was merely his understanding of how the righteousness of God would be satisfied; if we have moved beyond the cosmological explanation to a political and social one, the principle is the same: the justice of God is still served.

When we find the Gospel in the garb of the cosmological metaphysicis of another era, there is once again no sense in describing this as mythological and childish as seen from the plateaus of modern times. Behind this theistic representation of the world into which the kerygma enters, stands a real affliction of mankind; his suffering in chaos, in the absurdity of history, and the threat of transiency. The doctrine of the two natures was not ontological speculation. It was the Christian answer of freedom to the agony of transiency. Behind that cosmological representation of

1. Jürgen Moltmann, *Theology of Hope*, trans. J. W. Leitch (London: SCM Press, 1967), p. 16.

the world stands the question of theodicy, the question of suffering in expectation of God's just world. If that theistic representation of the world is outdated today, this interrogation of God about evil and pain is still not relegated to the past. The question has merely lost its old cosmological form. It has become more of a political and social question. Therefore this cosmological theology can develop into a political theology, because "politically" (in the broadest sense of the word) mankind suffers and struggles against, but also brings forth, evil. One can, of course, demythologize the answers of the fathers; but he cannot demythologize the foundation of the painful question which they wanted to answer. The old apocalyptical, world-historical eschatology has losts its cosmological language, but its lasting horizon is the theodicy question.[2]

It is perhaps less than adequate even to speak of *revolution,* Moltmann has pointed out, for the word originated as an astronomical term which indicated a return to an earlier position. What the Christian faith is about is more like *provolution,* a going forward to a position where we have never been. As Rosemary Ruether says, Moltmann's God is not primordial but eschatological; it is not so important that he stands at the beginning of the process as that he stands at the end of it! Thus Moltmann is able to speak of an ontological shift from being mere creatures in the created order to becoming the sons of God, and to say that the ontological ambivalence of the *creatio ex nihilo* is ultimately overcome in the *participatio in Deo.*[3]

There is one strikingly important thing, it occurs to me, about the kind of neoeschatological theology Moltmann represents.

It facilitates the gathering of all our secular-salvationist ideologies—education, technology, personality, community planning, revolution, etc.—under the umbrella of the Christian faith. This is highly significant because, while most of us are not disposed to hail any of them as the single panacea for which mankind has long

2. Jürgen Moltmann, "Toward a Political Hermeneutics of the Gospel," in Peerman and Marty, eds., op. cit., p. 83.
3. Ibid., p. 89.

been waiting, neither are we quite prepared to dismiss them as having no relation to our quest for redemption. They *are* related. Even the most dedicated of evangelicals must reserve some place of respect deep in his psyche for them. We *know*, without knowing quite how we know, that they have to do with the wholeness of man and the re-creation of the world.

If we can do what Moltmann asks—namely, adjust our spectacles to view salvation as an eschatological process in which we participate—then we have a framework *within the Christian faith and the Christian community* for attacking the problems of society and praying for the secular consummation of the divine will. And the struggle itself then helps to produce the Christian community. We achieve our identities as individuals and the Church achieves its identity as a community when we identify with Christ and the work he both clarified and provided a major impetus for. We no longer flounder in a purposeless, passionless existence. Our direction clear, we find ourselves suddenly, almost mystically, infused with new life and energy.

The secret, of course, is that Moltmann holds, despite his emphasis on change and adaptation, to the centrality of Christ's death and resurrection for our faith. The death roots us in the realities of evil and intransigence in the world; the resurrection symbolizes transformation and triumph over even the realities.

Zen Buddhism speaks of a "net of jewels" when it tries to describe all the truths there are; each reflects the light like a gem, and the light from all truths becomes a single effulgence. Alan Watts describes the "liberated man" *(jivanmukta)* of Buddhism this way: "He sees the world that we see; but he does not mark it off, measure it, divided it in the same way. He does not look upon it as really or concretely broken down into separate things and events."[4]

4. Alan Watts, *The Way of Zen* (Harmondsworth, Eng.: Penguin Books, 1962), p. 60.

We are no more able than the Buddhist to mark off the ways to salvation: they are innumerable. They are our "net of jewels." Yet the radiance of Christ—his life, teachings, death, resurrection, and presence—"draws" all other light and, uniting with it, bestows on it an intensity it would otherwise lack. We cannot arrogantly say that no man can be saved apart from him; the arrogance is worse than foolishness. But for those who accept his lordship in the light of the eschatological process, he does provide a sense of integration which even those who believe in Man may feel to be missing in their lives.

The reason for this is that, while he is Man, he also reminds us, in a way more recent secular ideologies do not, that our becoming Man is willed out before us by a power not our own. We are drawn on, irresistibly, by something acting in our behalf. Even when we fail, when monstrous wars break out and foul murders are done in secret places, we do not despair, but intensify our efforts to join forces with that higher power and help to hasten its day in our world. We do not lack an appreciation for the thickness and depth of the darkness entrenched in our land and in our very selves; but we lift up our hearts, because a voice comes from beyond and speaks ever of rolling it back, even to the point, incomprehensible, of dispelling it forever!

## Love and Revolution

Dale Brown, in *The Christian Revolutionary,* remarks upon the way Christ *as Man* provides the real basis of the revolutionary ideal.

It is only when one has a high vision of what man should be that he can be impatient with the way man is. And it is only through a concrete experience with good men—or an "ideal" man—that we are convicted of how much less than really human most of us actually are. Through such a picture of the new humanity, one is freed to love man for what he might become instead of for what he is. It is this christological or theological basis for humanism that may claim to make possible a more radical humanism, one that enables us to love even the unlovely.[5]

Brown has put his finger on the thing that most distinguishes the "radical humanism" of Christianity: its emphasis on love. There are many versions of the apocalyptic vision besides the Christian one. But the difference—the *profound* difference—between the Christian version and all the others is its model of laying down one's life for others.

This is the genius, we are bound to say, of the Johannine emphasis in the New Testament. Receiving an apocalyptic tradition sealed by the death and resurrection of Christ, yet threatened by the inexplicable delay of his expected return, those who gave us the Fourth Gospel and the Epistles of John perceived and illuminated the greatest human truth in the entire Jesus episode: that a man, in order to bring in the age of apocalyptic fulfillment for all mankind, would lay down his life in a cruel and horrible death. No higher motivation for revolution could ever be conceived. This one puts to shame all those having to do only with self-aggrandizement, with the overthrow of tyranny for one's own immediate gains of wealth, power, or well-being.

An illustration of its continuing power may be seen in the acts and words of Daniel Berrigan, who is considered an insurrectionist by a government not yet programed to judge of acts of love and altruism. Berrigan says, in *They Call Us Dead Men:*

The greatest changes within human life thus come to pass when a man has awakened to the existence of his brethren. And when we come to think of our own times, we must take heart that such an awakening is actually occurring all around us, in the most unexpected places and in lives one would have placed least hope in. What a momentous thing it

5. Dale W. Brown, *The Christian Revolutionary,* (Grand Rapids, Mich.: William B. Eerdmans Co., 1971), p. 72

is that Christians who are willing to spend themselves for their brethren need never stand alone.[6]

Governments cannot capitulate to acts of anarchy. It is not time, and they are not ready. But it is the gratuitous acts of Berrigans and Kings and others that call the status quo into judgment and inch us closer and closer to the time when they will be ready.

Eldridge Cleaver said in *Soul on Ice* that rape is an insurrectionary act. That may be true. But there is no power in the world more revolutionary than love, and no act more revolutionary than dying for another. This is so because love breaks the circuits of predictability in men. We say there are certain needs and desires pent up in the human psyche; if we study those needs and program the environment to satisfy them, even barely and at the most critical moments, we can control mankind in almost limitless tyranny. But love defies such a program. It does not react according to need and desire. It behaves spontaneously, erratically, unexpectedly. Which of us is able to say today that tomorrow he might offer his life in behalf of another, or of many others—?

I am not competent to measure the achievement of Norman O. Brown's *Love's Body*. It is a great Joycean, Brobdingnagian prose-poem meditation on Freudian mysticism. But the line of Brown's thinking is clear: the world hurtles on toward its destiny of fulfillment, in which mind and body will be perfectly fused. What it seeks is unity, union, the oneness of all, and the unmistakable sign of what it seeks is the Christ who dies and is made alive. Brown speaks of "the erotic sense of reality" which drives us toward unification. This sense, he says, discovers early the inadequacy of mere fraternity or brotherhood as a means of reunification. We must be "far more deeply unified, or not at all." The true form of unification, says Brown, is: "we are all members of one body."

6. Daniel Berrigan, *They Call Us Dead Men: Reflections on Life and Conscience* (New York: The Macmillan Co., 1968), p. 107.

"The true form of the unification of the human race is not the brothers, Cain and Abel, but Adam the first man, and Christ the second man: for as in Adam all die, even so in Christ shall all be made alive."[7]

History thus is "the history of one man." We rise from *history* to *mystery*—from shadows to reality. The only prayer is for the end of the world. And "the real meaning of the last days is Pentecost." Pentecost—where all men become one in the spirit of Christ, and had all things common, even language. And it is all predicated, from first to last, on the willing death of the self in order that the Other might live!

## Love and Planning

We cannot, however, merely trust to Providence that the reunification (or unification, if we prefer to say it has never existed before) will occur. Perhaps it would, but we cannot wait upon that. As Christ is our model, having died for us and the apocalyptic hope in our behalf, we are called to extend his action by undertaking similar positions of altruism in our own day. Our cosmological expectancies may differ from his, so that we do not look for one death or even one war to transform the world-home; but we share without diminution his confidence that it does contribute to an ultimate transformation.

As Moltmann says,

The coming lordship of the risen Christ cannot be merely hoped for and awaited. This hope and expectation also sets its stamp on life, action and suffering in the history of society. Hence mission means not merely propagation of faith and hope, but also historic transformation of life. The life of the body, including also social and public life, is expected as a sacrifice in day-to-day obedience (Rom. 12. 1 ff.). Not to be conformed

7. Norman O. Brown, *Love's Body* (New York: Vintage Books, 1966), pp. 82–83.

to this world does not mean merely to be transformed in oneself, but to transform in opposition and creative expectation the face of the world in the midst of which one believes, hopes and loves. The hope of the gospel has a polemic and liberating relation not only to the religions and ideologies of men, but still more to the factual, practical life of men and to the relationships in which this life is lived. It is not enough to say that the kingdom of God has to do only with persons; for one thing, the righteousness and peace of the promised kingdom are terms of relationship and accordingly have to do also with the relationships of men to each other and to things, and secondly, the idea of an a-social human personality is an abstraction. The reason why Christian hope raises the "question of meaning" in an institutionalized life is, that in fact it cannot put up with these relationships and sees the "beneficial unquestioningness of life" in them only as a new form of vanity and death.

It is in fact in search of "other institutions," because it must expect true, eternal life, the true and eternal dignity of man, true and just relationships, from the coming kingdom of God. It will therefore endeavour to lead our modern institutions away from their own immanent tendency towards stabilization, will make them uncertain, historify them and open them to that elasticity which is demanded by openness towards the future for which it hopes. In practical opposition to things as they are, and in creative reshaping of them, Christian hope calls them in question and thus serves the things that are to come. With its face towards the expected new situation, it leaves the existing situation behind and seeks for opportunities of bringing history into ever better correspondence to the promised future.[8]

This is a vision of Christianity not only tenable in the contemporary world but highly attractive and exciting. It holds at its center the "new" act of Christ for the historical realization of the Kindgom of God, refusing to blink away the gritty realities of conflict, suffering, and death. Instead of retreating from the noise of battle

---

8. Moltmann, *Theology of Hope,* pp. 329–30. This statement is, in my opinion, much clearer and more emphatic than any in the author's other book on the subject of *Hope and Planning* (London: SCM Press, 1971).

for the temporary peace of the cloister or the fantasized hope of a better life in "the world to come," it actually joins the battle and forces the issue of a better life now—not for the believer himself, but for all God's "little ones." Its world to come is a world to come *here,* reaffirming the essential Hebraic understanding all along that the earth is good, not evil, and dealing a resounding blow to the head of that ancient Gnostic heresy: that matter is evil and to be fled for the soul's everlasting welfare.

This is not to deny the possibility of an afterlife. There are ancient and perhaps wise presentiments which seem to warrant somehow at least a part of the speculations of "heavenly theologians" and psychic phenomenalists; I have no quarrel with these. But I do reject, categorically, the escapist tendency to locate eternal life on some other plane of existence than the one we presently occupy, so that the old question "If God is good and all-powerful, why did he permit the death of Jesus?" must be raised again and again with frustrating unanswerability. Obviously he is good but not all-powerful—at least not in any sense that would render us mere automata—and Christ was consciously leading the way for his power-play against the Enemy. If the power-play did not come off entirely, it did so partially, and is still coming off, so long as men and women realize it is doing so and commit themselves to leading the way for it.

There is an unforgettable picture of how this works in Alan Paton's beautiful novel *Cry, the Beloved Country.* Absalom Kumalo, son of Reverend Stephen Kumalo, a native South African, it will be recalled, shot and killed Arthur Jarvis, the son of a white landowner. It is a double tragedy, for both fathers have loved their sons. The elder Jarvis reads and ponders a manuscript his son was working on; it speaks of the hypocrisy of Christianity in a land where white men hinder the advance of black men and economic considerations cancel out ethical ideals. He goes to meet Kumalo, the father, and they take refuge from the rain in a native church.

He asks if the boy has been reprieved. Kumalo, with trembling hands, extracts a letter from his purse; the execution will be on the fifteenth of the month. Jarvis stares at the cross on the altar, and says he will remember.

Before the fifteenth, Jarvis's wife dies. Kumalo sends his sympathy. Jarvis writes back to thank him and to say that it was one of his wife's last wishes that he help the natives to build a new church at Ndotsheni; he will come to discuss it later.

But it isn't a church alone that he builds. The people at Ndotsheni have been starving because the land has been dry for years and they have no modern methods of agriculture. Jarvis sends a great earthmover, and a dam is thrown up to catch the rains. The people begin to have hope again. Eventually there will be grain and cattle. The young men will no longer go away. Old and young will have milk to drink.

A new spirit of life moves among the people like an electric current. There is nothing yet, but there is much to talk about in the huts. "Although nothing has come yet, something is here already."

On the fourteenth, Kumalo goes up into the mountain. He has gone twice before—once when the child Absalom was deathly ill and once when he was greatly tempted to leave the ministry to manage a store for a white man who promised him much money.

He sleeps fitfully, wondering each time he awakens whether the boy is awake and what he is feeling.

Once he cries out, "Oh, my son, my son!"

At four in the morning, he positions himself to watch for the sun's rising, when it will be done. Setting the maize cakes and tea his wife has given him on a stone, he gives thanks, eats the cakes, and drinks a little tea. Then he prays deeply and earnestly, raising his eyes between petitions to look to the east. As the dawn begins to break, he removes his hat and places it on the ground. Rising to his feet, he clasps his hands before him, and stands thus until the sun is in the sky.

There is no separating these stands: they belong together. A violent death, a Christian legacy, two fathers who suffer, each in his own manner, but resolve to make the earth more habitable for others. Life is like that—tangled, complicated, frustrating, filled with sorrow. But that isn't all! There is a dream—a dream of wholeness, of unity, of men dwelling together in peace and love. And the two of them—the frustration and the dream—are brought together in the Cross.

Love becomes part of the planning.

## The Salvation Tree

I commented in the beginning of this book on Beckett's *Waiting for Godot* and its withered tree—Yggdrasill, Bo-tree, Cross—which presides as the only backdrop for the play. In the second and final act it has acquired "four or five" leaves—presumably left to the discretion of the prop manager. These are still hardly enough to qualify the tree for much resemblance to the great Tree of Life of which the scriptures speak, conjuring up an image of abundant leafiness and vitality.

And the characters don't really identify it with redemption of any kind—except once, perhaps, when they attempt to hang themselves from it.

But Beckett was not through with the image, or his characters weren't. In a subsequent play, called *Endgame,* it enters again. Or almost enters.

*Endgame* is even sparer than *Godot.* The world seems to be at an end of some sort, though not quite. Clov, the one character who is able to move about, looks out through the single aperture on the stage, and reports that everything is "corpsed." Hamm, his companion, occupies a wheelchair, and Hamm's parents reside in two large dustbins, which they never leave, at the side of the stage.

They are glad the world is going to die. In fact, their only fear is that something might get it started up again—a rodent or a cockroach or something—and Clove is extra watchful for any signs of life, lest it happen.

Once there is a bit of excitement when Clove sees, or thinks he sees, something moving. It may be a small boy.

The careful listener remembers Hamm's tale about a dirty-faced man who came to him once on Christmas Eve and talked about his son in some distant place. Would Hamm take the son in? And later the man occurs to Hamm again, and Hamm says he had wanted work as a gardener, but Hamm wouldn't have him because he had a son, and the son *would climb the trees*——

The references are unmistakable. Hamm was talking about Christ and the Cross.

But now the tree is only a fleeting mental image and lacks even the tangibility of the tree in *Godot*. It is Beckett's way: he pushes everything through smaller and smaller openings until it recedes to the point of vanishing. The title *"Endgame"* is itself significant: in chess, it is the stage of the game when there are so few pieces on the board that a stalemate results and the players face only the prospect of endless moving back and forth.

Beckett has lost all sense of revolution, says Marcuse; he is ready to make an end of everything and let literature be only literature, serving no further purpose.[9]

He may be right, though this is not the place to argue it. I am more concerned for two things that seem to abide in Beckett's thought: first, the inseparability of man and the image of the Cross —the tramps in *Godot* can't get away from the tree, and Hamm in *Endgame* can't forget the man with the son who would have climbed the trees; second, the idea that at the Cross/tree everything may get "started up" again! Maybe it is little more than a premonition, but I have the feeling that Becket has *not* lost all

9. Herbert Marcuse, "Art and Revolution," *Partisan Review* (Spring 1972), p. 179.

sense of revolution. On the contrary, I believe the revolution can be felt to pulse beneath everything he has written. What is on the surface is desiccated and brittle, to be sure; it is a depressing picture of the end of man in our time. Beckett is *the* dramatist of ecological apocalypse. Life can ebb no lower than it is seen in his plays and novels.

Yet *underneath*—below the surface—something moves. Eerily, uncannily, it moves. The allusions to desire, to primeval forests, to beasts, to sexuality, to blood-religion, are like a rustling in the leaves.

When one waits with Becket and listens—listens to the night, to the void, to one's own breathing—one hears something like a distant rumble, maybe an earthquake, cosmological, about to tear through everything, through the thin, dry surface, and establish a new order, with new mountains and new plains, and new seas, and new rivers running to the seas, and maybe—yes—new trees by the rivers.

I think I have heard that in Beckett.

And I think it is time.


"Then he showed me the river of the water of life, sparkling like crystal, flowing from the throne of God and of the Lamb down the middle of the city's street. On either side of the river stood a tree of life, which yields twelve crops of fruit, one for each month of the year. The leaves of the trees serve for the healing of the nations, and every accursed thing shall disappear. The throne of God and of the Lamb will be there, and his servants shall worship him; they shall see him face to face, and bear his name on their foreheads. There shall be no more night, nor will they need the light of lamp or sun, for the Lord God will give them light; and they shall reign for evermore." (Rev. 22:1–5)

73 74 75 76 77 10 9 8 7 6 5 4 3 2 1